A Call from Hell

The True Story of Larry Gene Bell a Small-Town Monster and the Crime that Shook the Nation

True Crime Explicit Volume 10

Genoveva Ortiz, True Crime Seven

TRUE CRIME Z

Copyright © 2023 by Sea Vision Publishing, LLC

All Rights Reserved.

No part of this publication may be reproduced, distributed, or transmitted in any form or by any means, including photocopying, recording, electronic or mechanical methods, without the prior written permission of the publisher, except in the case of brief quotations embodied in critical reviews and certain other non-commercial uses permitted by copyright law.

Much research, from a variety of sources, has gone into the compilation of this material. We strive to keep the information up-to-date to the best knowledge of the author and publisher; the materials contained herein is factually correct. Neither the publisher nor author will be held responsible for any inaccuracies. This publication is produced solely for informational purposes, and it is not intended to hurt or defame anyone involved.

ISBN: 9798872562184

Table of Contents

Table of Contents 5

Introduction 11

I The Abduction 13

II The Search Continues 22

III The Letter 34

IV The Profile 39

V The Calls 45

VI The Terror 58

VII The Request 65

VIII The Discovery 75

IX The End of the Search 80

X The Calls Continue 89

XI The Funeral 128

XII The Next Girl 139

XIII The Next Discovery *145*

XIV The Break at Last *153*

Conclusion *163*

References *165*

Acknowledgements *167*

I A Monster on the Loose *171*

About True Crime Seven *179*

Explore the Stories of
The Murderous Minds

A Note

From True Crime Seven

Hi there!

Thank you so much for picking up our book! Before you continue your exploration into the dark world of killers, we wanted to take a quick moment to explain the purpose of our books.

Our goal is to simply explore and tell the stories of various killers in the world: from unknown murderers to infamous serial killers. Our books are designed to be short and inclusive; we want to tell a good scary true story that anyone can enjoy regardless of their reading level.

That is why you won't see too many fancy words or complicated sentence structures in our books. Also, to prevent typical cut and dry style of true crime books, we try to keep the narrative easy to follow while incorporating fiction style storytelling. As to information, we often find ourselves with too little or too much. So, in terms of research material and content, we always try to include what further helps the story of the killer.

Lastly, we want to acknowledge that, much like history, true crime is a subject that can often be interpreted differently. Depending on the topic and your upbringing, you might agree or disagree with how we present a story. We understand disagreements are inevitable. That is why we added this note so hopefully it can help you better understand our position and goal.

Now without further ado, let the exploration to the dark begin!

Introduction

YOU NEVER THINK IT WILL HAPPEN TO YOU.

Countless people love true crime. They love the mystery, the drama, and all the gory details. For many, true crime is little more than grim entertainment, but for some unlucky few, the pain is very, very real.

In 1985, Lexington County, part of Columbia, South Carolina, was a quiet community. Most people knew each other. Churchgoers formed strong, tight-knit communities. Within that group were the Smiths, an average, unassuming family with two beautiful daughters.

Murder, kidnapping—it was the kind of stuff that only happened in movies. No one could have ever anticipated that one of the girls would become the victim of a crime.

But nobody is ever as safe as they think they are. Evil lurks everywhere, hidden by the ability to appear like anyone else.

This book covers the abduction of Shari Faye Smith, the disturbing harassment campaign waged against her family, and the FBI's race to catch the suspect before he could strike again.

I
The Abduction

IT WAS A SWELTERING HOT DAY, OVER ONE hundred degrees, when Sharon "Shari" Faye Smith was taken. The date was May 31, 1985, the tail-end of spring, but living in Southern Carolina meant that summer came early. In spite of the heat, Shari had had a busy day. With her high school graduation just two days away, followed by a class trip to the Bahamas, she found herself busy preparing for a new stage of life. She had spent the morning doing the daily prayer she always shared with her family before heading off to rehearse with her chorus teacher, as she had been selected to sing "The Star-Spangled Banner" at the commencement ceremony alongside a classmate. After a much-needed pool party at a friend's house, she was more than ready to head home for the day.

She had no idea that, within a tiny, seemingly insignificant window of time, an unknown predator had already set his sights on her.

Still clad in her swimsuit, she drove her blue Chevette to the Smith family home located at 5700 Platt Springs Road of Lexington, a suburb of the state's capitol city. The house had been built in the center of a vast plot of land, leaving all four sides surrounded by what was, at this time of year, a sea of drying grass save for the swimming pool in the back. The pathway from the mailbox to the front door was around seven hundred feet, but it was a distance Shari had grown used to crossing.

Before she did so again, however, she needed to check the mail.

Shari opened the mailbox and took out a few letters. She hardly had the chance to look at them when she heard a car pull up behind her. A man she did not recognize looked at her with hungry eyes from the driver's seat. He said something she could not hear over the sound of both cars' engines still running.

The man did not bother to repeat himself. Instead, he hurried out of the car, closing the space between him and Shari in the blink of an eye. He grabbed her, and to Shari's horror, pressed what she soon realized was the cold metal barrel of a gun to her body. If she wanted to live, he warned her, then she better get in his car.

Shari had a righteous upbringing and had been raised to see the best in everyone. In all her innocence, she likely had no idea what fate awaited her when she stepped into the car. When he drove off, did she understand that she would never return?

But what is known for certain is that her father Bob Smith, a Baptist pastor and engineer, had been the first person to notice that something was amiss. He and his wife, Hilda, had been out back by the pool around the time their daughter arrived. When he first saw her car parked at the end of their driveway, he had assumed she had merely stopped to pick up the mail. When he looked out the window a while later, however, he saw the car still there, unmoved. Hilda tried to soothe his worries by offering the possibility that Shari was reading a letter sent by Dawn, the eldest Smith sister, and got caught up because the two were very close, but a sinking feeling came over him.

Bob hurried outside to his own car and drove down to check on his daughter. His worst fears were realized.

Shari was gone. Her car was running and all her belongings, including her shoes, were still inside. A handful of letters were strewn across the ground, indicating that she had dropped them suddenly, and perhaps unwillingly. He could make out her bare footprints leading away from the front seat, but none were leading back. Worst of all was what he found in her purse: her medication.

Shari Faye suffered from a rare medical condition: diabetes insipidus, more commonly known as "water diabetes." It meant that Shari's body had a hard time regulating fluids and could quickly become dehydrated, something that, given the intense heat, could quickly put her in serious danger without her medicine.

Panicked, Pastor Smith hurried back inside the house to get to Hilda. He told his wife that her car had still been running but she was not in it.

Mrs. Smith was understandably just as worried. While her husband called the police, she hopped into her own car and drove around in search of Shari. It pained her to have to return to the house without her and endure the half-hour wait before help arrived. All Hilda could do at the moment was pace around the property, praying silently for her daughter's safety.

In South Carolina today, there is no amount of time required before a family can report a person missing. This was unfortunately not the case for many states in previous decades. Had Shari been anyone else, it is likely the authorities would have needed to wait before beginning their search, considering the fact that she was right on the brink of adulthood. The fact that Shari was a diabetic without her medicine, however, created a sense of urgency that got police to act right away. What followed was one of the largest searches conducted in the history of Lexington County.

Air teams were called in to conduct aerial searches. The governor's office's Emergency Preparedness Division arrived to set up tractor-trailer's that would serve as a base for the investigation. These trailers were full of all sorts of equipment, including telephones, radios, and cameras, that could keep the place running twenty-four hours a day.

Authorities were eager to help not just because of the urgency of Shari's health needs, but also because they were already familiar enough with the Smiths to know it was unlike the girl to have run away.

"She's not a runaway," Captain Bob Ford of the sheriff's department told the press. "We can't accept any theories that she ran away from home."

The efforts were led by Lexington County Sheriff James R. Metts, who also set up base in a trailer near the Smith home. The plan was for this place to remain accessible at all hours in case any new information regarding Shari or her abductor came in. Having everything in one place meant that they could save precious time—Shari's time.

They would need the public's help. Whenever something strange happened in a small town, word got around fast. Soon after, calls came in from locals reporting sightings of suspicious vehicles. Two men who had driven past the Platt Springs Road just after three in the afternoon claimed to have seen Shari standing at the mailbox. At the same time, a car, described as being reddish-purple or maroon in color, was coming up the opposite side of the road, headed directly towards the Smith home. Based off of their brief sighting, the men believed the other vehicle to be an Oldsmobile Cutlass, possibly a model from 1982 to 1984. The driver appeared to be a man in his thirties.

When they passed by, they looked in their rear-view mirror. The taillights of the Oldsmobile came on. The vehicle had come to a stop at the mailbox.

A short while later, the two men passed by the Smith home again. This time, they saw Shari's Chevette, but they did not see Shari.

With no luck that first day, the search carried on into the weekend, expanding to over a hundred volunteers combing the area, undaunted by the heat. Helicopters and bloodhounds were used. The phone at the Smith family house was wiretapped. Still, no progress was made aside from the recovery of a red bandanna belonging to Shari. It was located on the side of the road less than a mile from the house, and law enforcement believed that she may have dropped it from a moving vehicle, a sort of breadcrumb in her kidnapper's path, but unfortunately it did not lead to further clues.

It had been a long and hard day. They had combed through about twenty miles of land with almost nothing to show for it. At least two volunteers fainted from heat exhaustion. Another man stepped on a nail while a police officer suffered a nasty spider bite. They were all taken to the Lexington County Hospital by an ambulance that had been kept at the scene in case of emergencies.

When the search concluded for the day just before six in the evening, the temperature still hovered over ninety-seven degrees. Everyone was in need of rest, though the Sheriff asked them to return early the next morning before the worst of the heat.

Past experience with similar crimes led the South Carolina Law Enforcement Division (commonly abbreviated as SLED in sources) to expect a ransom demand to come in soon. As grim as the prospect that Shari was being held for ransom was, it was actually the preferable situation than most alternatives, because ransom demands meant the perp was likely to communicate with law enforcement and being able to communicate with a perp made it easier to catch them. It also meant it would have been more likely that Shari would have been kept alive as a bargaining chip– that is, if they were lucky. When the third day came with no demand, the local authorities were unsure what to do next.

It was clear that this was no ordinary case. It was something bigger than their resources could handle on their own, so they needed help. Word of Shari's abduction soon reached the FBI in the Colombia, South Carolina field office.

II

The Search Continues

DESPITE THE COMMON PUBLIC PERCEPTION on kidnappings, abduction by a stranger is rare. In a 1985 article for *The Denver Post*, "Hysteria Inflates Estimates of Missing Children : Oft-Quoted Figures Exaggerated, Law Enforcement Officials and Experts Say" writers Diana Griego and Louis Kilzer shed light on what child abduction statistics were actually like: "Various groups warn us that as many as 1.5 million children disappear each year and that strangers kidnap as many as 50,000 of them. And, the groups say, as many as 4,000 children are murdered after being abducted.

However, law enforcement officials, joined by leading missing-children experts, say that those numbers are grossly exaggerated.

One missing child is too many. The family tragedy of having a child kidnaped and murdered cannot be diluted by numbers of any kind.

Yet, the inflated numbers themselves are damaging the lives of millions of parents, affecting how they feel about their children's safety and what they should teach their children about the society they live in... The cases of children kidnaped by strangers on file with the FBI and children's groups show an even smaller number. The FBI reports that it had sixty-seven cases of children kidnaped by strangers in 1984. The National Center for Missing and Exploited Children says that it has firm records on one hundred forty-two cases."

Women and girls, particularly in close-knit communities with low crime rates like the one the Smith family lived in, are statistically far more likely to be taken by somebody they know. Griego and Kilzer write: "Law enforcement and missing children experts say that about 95% of missing children reports are on runaways, and most runaways return home within three days.

Most of the rest are children abducted in parental custody disputes. Only a small fraction are abducted by strangers." But who would want to hurt Shari or her parents? Shari's case was proving to be unprecedented in the area, something the likes of which local police had yet to have dealt with before.

Investigations into their backgrounds revealed that they were well-liked, had no enemies, or even any notable conflicts with anyone. Shari and her sister, Dawn, were quite popular; they were both known as local beauties with incredible talent when it came to music. They had dreams of someday making it big on the Christian music scene, a goal that everyone who knew them believed was within their grasp.

Perhaps all this positive attention was the reason Shari was targeted. Was there someone out there who was jealous of Shari to the point where they would want to get rid of her? Or maybe she had a fan who had grown to like her a little too much? After all, Pastor Smith ministered at local prisons, and sometimes he brought his daughters along to sing for the inmates. Who knew what sort of dangerous person they could have come into contact with in the past? Either way, the case was not looking good, and the fact that authorities could not yet narrow in on any suspects made it more difficult for them to decide on their next steps.

In the meantime, there was nothing more the Smiths could do but pray and wait. It was a particularly difficult time for Dawn. She had literally just returned to her apartment in Charlotte from a shopping trip to buy a graduation gift for her little sister when she had gotten the news. It was her roommate who relayed the message. "Shari's been abducted," she said. "You need to call your mom."

At first, Dawn was more confused than worried. What did she mean "Shari's been abducted"? Why would anybody do that? Besides, crimes like that only happened in movies, not in real life, and especially not to the people she knew. When Dawn called her mother, she was half-expecting to hear that there had been some mistake, that her roommate had misheard, but there was no error.

Instead, her mother confirmed it. "You need to pack a bag. A patrolman is coming to pick you up at your apartment."

Dawn still did not quite understand. "Mom, I can't come home! My show opens tomorrow. I've got to be at the show. I'm sure Shari is fine." At the time, Dawn was employed by the Carowinds amusement park as a country singer and dancer, a job that Shari had been hoping to join her at during the coming summer.

"No, this is real. Pack a bag," Hilda reiterated. "They'll be there in ten minutes."

Just as Hilda said, a policeman soon came knocking at her door. Dawn grabbed her belongings and followed, albeit with some reluctance, to the patrol car. She left the gift she had purchased—a hamster named Peachy—behind, and as the cop drove on for two hours in grim silence, she began to wonder if Shari would ever even get to receive it.

Dawn had not been the only Smith child who had been abruptly called to the home. The youngest sibling, their brother, Robert, had also been dropped off by friends as soon as they got the word out. Also in attendance was their paternal grandmother, aunts and uncles, and finally, Shari's boyfriend, Richard. They all gathered in the living room and held hands.

Pastor Smith led the prayer. "God, we know that while we don't know where Shari is, we know that You know where she is, and we're going to trust You to watch over her. We're going to look to You to bring her home and get us through this."

Though it helped ease their spirits to be surrounded by friends and family, Dawn was having a hard time dealing with it all. As she was so close to Shari, she was among the very first people to be questioned about the disappearance. Police already knew that it was unlikely that Shari ran away on her own, and they hoped that Dawn could provide any background knowledge that may be useful in figuring out what exactly happened that Friday. In a private interview by SLED agent Lydia Glover, Dawn offered whatever she knew about Shari's life in recent times.

There was nothing negative she could report on Shari or their family. The only thing she could think of is that there was, during a few occasions, Shari had gotten frustrated with their father's strict rules and asked to stay with Dawn for a while. He could sometimes be a bit intimidating and overbearing, but he had never been abusive. In fact, there was no history of abuse in their immediate family at all, sexual, physical, or otherwise.

These tensions were always resolved. Shari was happy, as far as everyone who knew her believed, and she had so much to look forward to in the near future. There was no way she would have left it all behind.

Unfortunately, the alternative to a voluntary disappearance came with implications that were worse—far worse.

False hope arose when the family at last received a phone call demanding a ransom.

"I have Shari," said the stranger. "I want money, and I want you to put the Smith family's phone number on TV so I can talk to them. If you don't give me what I want, I'm gonna add Shari to the missing persons list." He wanted around two thousand dollars for Shari's return, but law enforcement was not taking the bait. After tracing the call to a nearby public phone booth, police spent hours waiting for the perp to return to the scene, hopefully to place further demands and get caught in the act. Frustratingly, this call turned out to be nothing more than a sick hoax perpetrated by Edward Robertson, a twenty-seven-year-old man with too much time on his hands and a desire for something that was not actually cash.

Four months earlier, Robertson had been released from prison. It had been far from his first stint; he had already faced five convictions with charges ranging from grand larceny to assault and battery. Now, he had no idea what to do with himself and his newfound freedom. In the time between that and the call, he had been working at an aluminum factory, and he was itching for his old life.

He asked local authorities if he could go back to prison, but they said the only way he could was if he committed another crime. The opportunity came right on time. He saw a news report about Shari missing and walked to a phone booth and called the Lexington County Sheriff's Department and told them he had her.

Robertson was arrested on Saturday, June 1st. He got his wish. He was held on a forty-one thousand dollar bond and later sentenced to five years in prison on charges of extortion, obtaining money under false pretenses, obstruction of justice, and making an obscene phone call.

This would not be the only hoax call the Smiths would receive, though the details of these later calls appear to have been far less extensively documented than Roberton's. The second hoax was placed on an unspecified date by eighteen-year-old Charles A. Allen, who had been convicted of breaking into and vandalizing a church earlier that year. Allen called the Smiths to offer knowledge of Shari's location in exchange for five hundred dollars. He also claimed to know the identities of three individuals involved with her abduction. Police, hoping for any possible leads, investigated, but the only thing to come from it was a waste of ten hours.

Tensions were understandably running high at the Smith home afterward. As the days went on, Dawn grew increasingly worried about her parents. She went into her father's office and found him seated at his desk chair. He looked shaken. He stated that he thought maybe Shari ran away because she could not measure up to Dawn's level. She did feel like she was compared to Dawn often.

Dawn was quite angry with her father, and as tears streamed down her face she wondered why her father would tell her something like this. Was he trying to blame her for Shari being gone? Had he considered that it was his overly strict ways that could have driven Shari away? Dawn held her tongue. Her father was hurting. All he wanted was to make sense of what had happened.

Although Dawn realized her father might have had a point, she acknowledged that Shari was a better singer than she was. Shari had a natural talent for singing whole-heartedly. But she always felt like she had to compete with Dawn. Shari had been happy and proud that Dawn had won singing competitions and had a performing job at Carowinds, but Shari often compared herself with Dawn, as younger sisters often tend to do.

Shari had had some hard breaks with her singing. Soon after being hired at Carowinds to sing and dance in the country show, she found out she had nodules on her vocal cords. She had to quit the show and remain quiet for six weeks on doctor's orders. It had been hard on all the family. Shari was heartbroken that she couldn't sing.

The Smiths were dealt a further blow on Sunday, June 2nd, the day of Shari's high school graduation, came and went without a word from her. To them, missing out on such an accomplishment was the final proof they needed to rule out any chance of her having gone willingly.

At last, the real breakthrough came during the very early hours of Monday, June 3rd.

It was around two in the morning when the phone rang. Bob Smith, still groggy from having woken so suddenly, answered it. The voice at the other end of the line asked to speak with his wife.

"I'm Mr. Smith," Bob clarified. "Can I help you?"

The voice would not budge. They would only talk to Hilda. When Hilda got on the line, the voice told her they wanted to talk to her about Shari. It appeared they had some rather important information to relay to the family. To prove that they were not just some other lowlife person looking for attention, they began to recount details that only the Smiths—or their daughter's kidnapper—would have known, such as what she had last been wearing when she vanished: a pair of white shorts over a swimsuit and black shoes that got left behind.

Hilda, who had understandably assumed that she had been speaking to a police officer or detective, confirmed these details. But then the voice said something that threw her for a loop: they asserted that authorities were looking for Shari in the wrong places.

They also told the Smith family to expect a letter from Shari in the mail that coming afternoon. It would contain specific details they should look out for such as the date, June 1st, 1985, as well as the time it has supposedly been written, ten after three in the morning, rounded off by two minutes. They also suggested, with little subtlety, that they ought to tell Sheriff Metts to go on the evening news and publicly call off the search.

Then the caller hung up.

As Hilda put the phone down, her mind and heart were racing. To her horror, she realized that this person had not been a member of law enforcement. They were the person who was holding her daughter captive.

But who were they? The voice had not been familiar to either her or her husband. It was a man's voice, they could tell that much, but there was something strange about it. It sounded as though it had been altered in some way.

Hilda was very upset when she told her daughter, Dawn, about the call, realizing the man who called probably had Shari.

It did not take authorities long to trace the phone call. They determined that it had been placed from a public payphone right outside C.D. Taylor's Grocery store, which was located just outside of town, a little over ten miles from the Smith home. Unfortunately, by the time police got to the scene, their perp was long gone. Searching the area for any clues such as fingerprints turned up nothing. It was like the man had never been there.

To police, this raised a terrifying possibility: this criminal was smart, and it was probably not his first crime, either.

III
The Letter

THE POSSIBILITY THAT THEY WERE DEALING with an experienced criminal was all the more reason for police to act fast. There was no point in waiting for the letter to arrive to the Smith family in the mail that afternoon when they could intervene before that. At around four in the morning, Sheriff Metts called Thomas Roof, the postmaster for Lexington County, and explained the urgency of the situation. Once they got Roof's permission to open the post office, two officers, J.E. Harris and Richard Freeman, set to work.

It proved to be a grueling task. Lexington is one of the largest counties in the state, and though its population in 1985 was about half of what it is today, that number was still well over one hundred thousand residents. Shari's letter was like a needle in a haystack, with a team of only three men to search among the seemingly endless mail.

Amazingly, they found the letter after three hours of sorting. It was a plain, unassuming-looking, white legal-sized envelope with no return address. The sender had addressed it simply to "the Smith family." The stamp used was that of a duck that, according to postmaster Roof, was still being sold at the time.

The men did not open the letter at this time. They believed it to be more appropriate for a member of Shari's family to do so, and quickly contacted Bob Smith. Even after Bob arrived, however, there were still additional precautions that needed to be taken.

County police as well as the FBI agents involved were still trying to determine exactly what kind of criminal they were dealing with here. So far, they had determined that he was calculating and meticulous; the fact that he was willing to call the family himself told them that he likely had a sadistic streak, but the fact that he went through the effort of electronically disguising his voice also meant that he was not stupid enough to blow his cover for the thrill of it. Their alleged kidnapper likely had some background knowledge of electrical engineering, but did he have other skills he could use to his advantage? What if he had the resources to place something very dangerous within the envelope?

Now with gloves on, the officers very carefully removed the letter from the envelope and transferred it to a transparent folder. This was in order to preserve it as much as it was to protect themselves. If there was anything on this letter they could use—fingerprints, hair, microscopic traces of blood—they needed to make sure they kept it, so much so that they would not even read the original letter directly. Instead, photocopies were made and later shared with other officers.

The letter was actually two pages in length, written on lined yellow paper, the kind you might use when taking notes. The style of handwriting was positively identified as being Shari's. She had written the phrase "GOD IS LOVE" on the first page. Right beneath that, she had drawn a heart as well as the phrase "ShaRichard," an obvious reference to her beloved boyfriend. It was a sweet message rendered both tragic and ominous by what followed on the next page: [These are the words of Shari Faye Smith there may be some errors.]

6/1/85 3:10AM I Love ya'll

LAST WILL AND TESTAMENT

I love you mommy, daddy, Robert, Dawn, & Richard and everyone else and all other friends and relatives. I'll be with my father now, so please, please don't worry! Just remember my witty personality & great special times we all shared together. Please don't let this ever ruin your lives and just keep living one day at a time for Jesus. Some good will come out of this. My thoughts will always be with you and in you!!

(casket closed)

I love you all so damn much. Sorry dad, I had to cuss for once! Jesus Forgive me! Richard Sweetie - I Really did & always will love You & treasure our special Moments. I ask one thing though, Accept Jesus as your personal savior. My family has been the greatest influence on my life. Sorry about the cruise money. Some body please go in my place.

Sorry if I ever disappointed you in any way, I only wanted to make you proud of me. Because I have always been proud of my family. Mom, dad, Robert & Dawn theres so much I want to say that I should have said before now. I love you!

I know y'all love me and will Miss me very much but if you'll stick together like we always did–y'all can do it! Please do not become hard or Upset. Everything works out for the Good of those who love the Lord.

All My Love Always–

I Love Ya'll

w/All My Heart!

Sharon (Shari) Smith

P.S. Nana–I love you so much. I kind of always felt like your favorite. You were mine.!

I Love You A Lot

Shari ended her last will and testament with a drawing of a smiley face.

IV
The Profile

ANY HOPES LAW ENFORCEMENT STILL HAD THAT Shari was being held for ransom—and that the kidnapper was somebody they could reason with—were completely dashed upon reading her letter. Shari had not been killed immediately after her abduction; her alleged kidnapper had allowed her to live long enough to write this letter—but that did not mean he was going to give her much more time after that. Police determined that, due to a lack of personal connection to Shari or her family, this was some sort of sexually motivated crime and continued to work creating a psychological profile of the criminal in question.

Special agent John Douglass, a member of the FBI's Columbia field office, was among those working on the case. True crime enthusiasts may recognize him as one of the authors behind the 1995 best-selling book: *Mindhunter: Inside the FBI's Elite Serial Crime Unit*, which later served as the inspiration behind the hit Netflix series of the same name. Douglas was a pioneer in the field of criminal profiling, and much of what we understand about the psychology behind violent crime has come from his work interviewing killers. He had even been able to develop a formula for criminal profiling: if he could figure out how the crime was committed plus why it was committed, he could eventually figure out who committed it.

It was grisly work, and taking on Shari's case was particularly difficult for Douglas, who had two young daughters of his own—but someone had to do it. The FBI would be working with local law enforcement to create a psychological profile of Shari's abductor. They needed to know exactly what kind of person they were dealing with in order to narrow in on a suspect and hopefully save precious time.

You may be surprised at the level of detail that criminal profilers can hypothesize from very little information. There are the obvious things first, such as the belief that Shari's abductor had prior criminal experience given the level of sophistication relative to what you might see from a "rookie" kidnapper. Not only did he manage to take Shari without anyone seeing, but he took careful measures to cover up his steps. He was bold enough to call the Smith family in the dead of night, but went to the effort of disguising his voice, something most people would not know how to do. He left no trace of himself, not even fingerprints, behind. He was a stickler for detail, and he liked to be in control. Clearly, this was a man who knew what he was doing, and that made him all the more dangerous.

In addition to being experienced, law enforcement deduced that this man likely had some sort of background in technology. Most likely, he had worked as an electrician at some point in his life. He was, they knew, male, and he was probably white as this sort of crime is usually not interracial. They believed he may have been under fifty years old, more specifically in his late twenties to late thirties. The unknown man was probably divorced or estranged from his spouse, and he may have had children who wanted little to do with him. His desire to control and dominate may have stemmed from feelings of insecurity in other aspects of his life; odds were that he felt he was not charming or attractive enough to approach a girl like Shari in the normal way. If he wanted her, he would have no other option than to take her by force.

Attempts to build a suspect profile didn't do much good when there were no actual suspects, however. There were millions of men who could have fit that description. For now, it was a waiting game, though it would not be long until the perp acted again.

Monday, June 2nd, was a rough day for the Smith family. The high school graduation that Shari had been working so hard towards came and went without a word, making what should have been a joyous event somber for the community. Monday's arrival meant the dawn of a new week without their beloved daughter and sister, a period of uncertainty that was proving to be longer than anyone had initially feared. Then, just after three in the afternoon, another phone call came in.

It was Dawn who picked up this time. "Hello?" she asked cautiously.

"Mrs. Smith?"

It was another disguised voice. Dawn instantly realized that this was the same man as before, the one who called them about the letter. Fear shot through her body, but she pressed on. "No, this is Dawn."

"I need to speak to your mother."

"Could I ask who is calling?"

"No," the voice replied simply.

"Okay, okay," said Dawn. "Hold on just a second, please."

A moment went by before Hilda took the receiver. "Hello?"

"Have you received the mail today?"

"Yes, I have."

"Do you believe me now?"

"Well, I'm not really sure I believe you because I haven't had any word from Shari, and I need to know that Shari is well."

"You'll know in two or three days," said the man.

"Why two or three days?"

He ignored the question. "Call off the search."

"Tell me if she is well," Hilda pleaded, her anxiety building. "Because of her disease. Are you taking care of her?"

Without another word, the caller hung up. The call was traced to a payphone outside a local pharmacy that was located a few miles from the house. Investigators rushed to the scene, but just as before, the caller was gone and left nothing, not even a single fingerprint, behind.

It was a short, frustrating call, but it seemed the caller was slowly giving investigators something to work with. Police had installed recording devices on the Smith family phone for this very purpose. Whether or not what the caller was giving could be useful to them, however, remained to be seen—and there were many more calls to come.

V
The Calls

THE SMITH FAMILY COULD NOT JUST GIVE IN TO the caller's demand to call off the search for Shari. That very same Monday afternoon, not long after the ominous phone call, the Smiths, alongside Sheriff Metts, made a television appearance for the local news. The family stood side by side, Bob Smith with an arm around his wife and an arm around his eldest daughter.

"Whoever has our daughter, Shari, we want her back," said Mr. Smith to the cameras. "We miss her. We love her. Please send her back home. She belongs here with us."

The goal of the interview was simple: to comfort Shari, if she was watching, or to appeal to the abductor's sense of empathy, if he had any. Unfortunately, it would appear that this goal would go unreached, but some good did come from the broadcast.

Mrs. Terri (spelled *Terry* by some sources) Butler, a housewife who lived in the area near the Smith home, had no idea she had witnessed a crime take place that scorching hot day back in late May. She had been driving down the road, as she often had, at around three thirty in the afternoon and just happened to see Shari pulling up to the Smith driveway in her blue Chevette. She had just passed the home when another car came racing by in the opposite direction. The driver, a white male, was clearly distracted and ended up merging onto the wrong lane—right towards Mrs. Butler's vehicle. He would have crashed into her had it not been for Mrs. Butler's quick thinking.

The driver had been leaning over in his seat, and his attention was focused on something beyond the road in front of him. Mrs. Butler honked her horn and he immediately snapped back and for a split second, their eyes met.

The incident may have ruffled the woman's feathers, but she had no reason to believe anything sinister had been happening. As she drove off to her destination, she took one look back at the other driver through her rearview mirror. His brake lights came on as he stopped beside Shari's Chevette. Then she went on about the rest of her day.

Mrs. Butler had not thought about that afternoon again until she saw the Smith family's desperate pleas on television, and she realized, with some horror, that she was a witness. She called the police and told them what she knew. They asked if she could recall what the driver had looked like. As brief as her glimpse of him had been, she could recall that he appeared to have been a white male. His hair was thin, and his hairline was either receding or he was already balding. His roundish face was clean shaven. With her assistance, law enforcement was finally able to create a composite sketch of the suspect.

That Monday was proving to be a long, eventful, and painful one for the Smith family. Just after eight in the evening, a call came in.

Dawn had been the first to get to it again this time. "Hello?" she asked.

"Dawn, did you come down from Charlotte?"

Her blood ran cold. It was their guy again. He must have seen the Smiths on television, having gone back to the media instead of giving up the search like he wanted. He must have been displeased with them, though strangely, his altered voice did not seem to betray any anger.

"Yes, I did," Dawn replied. "Who's calling, please?"

"I need to speak with your mother."

"Okay, she's coming."

"Tell her to hurry."

"She's hurrying. Tell Shari I love her."

He ignored this. Instead, he asked if the family had received the letter Shari wrote them.

"Yes, we did." Dawn paused to hand the receiver off. "Here's mother."

"Did you receive Shari Rae's letter?"

"Pardon? I can't hear you. It's not very clear. Speak louder."

"Did you receive the letter today?"

"Uh, yes. I did."

"Tell me one thing it said," he demanded. "Hurry."

"ShaRichard."

"What?"

"There was a little heart on the side," Hilda clarified. "ShaRichard. Written on the side."

"How many pages?"

"Two pages."

"Okay, and was it a yellow legal pad?"

"Yes."

"And on one side of the front page, it said 'Jesus is love.' Right?"

"No." Hilda could remember the contents of the terrible letter very clearly. "It said 'God is love.'"

"Well. God is love."

"Right."

"Okay. So now you know this is not a hoax call?"

"Yes, I know that."

"I'm trying to do everything possible to answer some of your prayers, so please, in the name of God, work with us here."

"Can you answer me one question, please? You... you are very kind and... and you seem to be a compassionate person and..." Hilda was struggling to get the words out, given the person she was speaking with. "And I think you know how I feel being Shari's mother and how much I love her. Can you tell me? Is she all right physically without her medication?"

"Shari is drinking a little over two gallons of water per hour and is going to the bathroom right afterward," he replied. "Well. Okay, now. This has gone too far. Please forgive me. Have an ambulance ready at any time at your house. And at Shari's request... she requests that only immediate family come and Sheriff Metts and the ambulance attendants. She don't want to make a circus out of this."

"Right. Okay."

"And where she said 'casket closed' in parentheses... If anything happens to her, she said her... one of her requests that she did not put there was to put her hands on her stomach. Cross her hands like she was praying in the casket."

"What now?"

"Cross her hands."

The odd statement alarmed Hilda. In this state, she may have misunderstood what he meant. "Why would anything happen to you? We don't want any harm to you. I... I promise... We just want Shari well and all right, okay?"

"Okay now," said the suspect. "Does Sheriff Metts realize this is not the hoax call?"

"Yes," she replied. "He knows this is not a hoax."

"Well, tell him to just forget all those suspects, and the only thing when I talk to you Monday morning, 2:30 in the morning the first time—"

"Yes. Yes, I did not realize. I thought you were a police officer."

"Okay, then listen. Listen real carefully. I've got to hurry. I know these calls are being traced, correct?"

"I do not know."

Okay. Now listen."

"I'm listening."

"Yeah, hold on a second," said the suspect. There was a pause.

"Are you still there?"

"Yes, okay. Just hold on a second."

"Uh, is Shari with you or can you tell me that?"

"I will not say," the caller replied.

"I can tell you're upset."

"Okay, now listen to us, please. Hold on before I forget it. You're all looking in the wrong place. Forget Lexington. Look in Saluda County. Do you understand?"

"Look in Saluda County?" she repeated.

"Exactly. Uh, closest to Lexington County within a fifteen-mile radius right over the line. Is that understood?"

"Yes."

The suspect went on. "Now please, and very, very soon, please... Now Shari's request. Shari Faye requests please no strangers hardly and when y'all... when we give the location—"

"No strangers," she confirmed. "Absolutely."

"Okay, now did you understand about the holding of the hands like she was in prayer in case something happens to us?"

"Yes, if something happens to y'all. But nothing... listen, nobody is going to harm you. I promise you that."

"Well, tell Sheriff Metts that he... I don't know what the problem is. I told you to forget looking around your house. Look in Saluda County."

"Listen," Hilda pleaded.

"Do you believe me now?" he asked.

"I believe you. There are so many people who love Shari—

"I know that."

"—and they just won't give up. They just continue to look."

That was when the caller made one of the most cryptic and unsettling statements to come out of the entire case. "I want to tell you... I want to tell you one other thing. Shari is now a part of me, physically, emotionally, mentally, and spiritually. Our souls are now one."

Hilda was understandably puzzled. "Your souls are now one with Shari?"

"Yes, and we're trying to work this out. So please do what we ask. You haven't been doing that. I don't understand, and she doesn't. And we sit here and we watch TV and we don't see no sheriff. We—"

"Why doesn't Shari talk to me? She... she knows me so well."

"That's why she asked me to communicate with you, not your husband. Aren't you aware of that?"

"Yes," said Hilda. "I know that. I know that she would ask you to talk with me."

But once again, he continued to talk past her. "And she said she does love y'all and like she said, do not let this ruin your lives."

"We're not going to let it ruin our... but listen, you tell Shari one thing."

"What is that?"

"There's no way my life could ever have any happiness in it again if Shari left this world with me bearing a guilt that I had failed in such a bad way, because I love her and I want to make her happy. I'll do anything—"

"She knows that."

"I'll do anything to work it out. She doesn't have to come home, okay? I'm serious. She does not have to come home. Anything."

"Uh, well, time up and... well, time's up. Please now have the ambulance ready at any time."

"At any time."

"This will not go any further and it will be soon."

"The ambulance... you're not telling me that something's going to happen to her and I'm going to have to have an ambulance?"

"No," he replied. "I'm telling you her condition."

Hilda could feel her fear spiking. "Is her condition getting bad? Is that what you're trying to tell me?"

"You know more about it than I do."

"I know I do and that's why I'm so worried about her!"

"Well, you just have the ambulance," he snapped. "And I'll tell you the location… and tell Sheriff Metts to get all his damn men in Saluda County. Okay? Well. God bless all of us."

"Will you call me soon?" Hilda asked.

"I will."

"Will you call me back tonight? I just need reassurance that she's still okay."

" I've got to be careful. I've got to go now and… and listen… Please, please, please forgive me for this. It just got out of hand."

"I know. Listen, do me one thing?"

"What is that?" he asked. "Hurry!"

"Just tell Shari… I know she knows how much I love her. Tell her. Tell her her daddy loves her, and her daddy will work anything out with her under the sun, and he admits we got a lot of problems, but we'll work them out… and her brother and sister love her. God bless you for taking care of my baby."

"Shari is protected, and like I said, she is a part of me now, and God looks after all of us. Good night."

"Good luck to you, too."

The call ended, and the police moved fast in hopes of catching their man this time. They managed to trace it to a payphone about eight miles from the Smith house, in front of a business called Wall Street Store off of Interstate 20 and Highway 204. Just as they feared, however, he was already gone, no trace of him left behind, like a ghost that now haunted them all.

VI
The Terror

IT HAD BEEN TRUE WHAT HILDA SAID ABOUT SO many people loving and caring about her daughter. Ever since word had gotten out about the abduction, the community had rallied together in support of the Smiths, and the help was much appreciated by the troubled family. They were seemingly on permanent high alert now, always waiting for any new phone calls from the suspect or any word from law enforcement. Understandably, the high tension left them all exhausted, and it was difficult to find the energy to care for their own needs. Thankfully, other family members, along with friends and volunteers, helped keep the Smiths, as well as police, fed as the search for Shari continued.

The kindness in these actions was evident, but it was just as clear now that the people of Lexington were as scared as they were sympathetic. Their immediate neighborhood had, up until recently, always been a safe one. Word of Shari Faye Smith's abduction had already become major news, with both the search and media coverage having spread across the entire state.

Change had come to their town in the worst way that May, even before the taking of Shari Smith. A horrific crime had taken place earlier that month, the day before Mother's Day.

For most readers, even those more well read in true crime, the name Marilee Whitten is unlikely to be a familiar one. Jeff Whitten, Marilee's older brother, wrote about the tragedy for the Bryan County News on its 34th anniversary: "...it was before the internet, and that's a blessing, I think. Stories are hard to find."

Like Shari, Marilee was only seventeen years old, still a child with the rest of her life to look forward to. Known simply as Lee by her friends and loved ones, the girl, who was once described as somewhat of a delinquent, was excited for the future. She had been eager to let go of her reputation as a trouble-maker and had made some big changes in the preceding months. When she had gotten hired as a pet groomer's assistant at a veterinary clinic, the young animal lover thought she lucked out, but what she really wanted was to pursue a career in law enforcement. Also, like Shari, Marilee had a steady boyfriend whom she adored.

But the biggest thing these two girls shared in common was being the unfortunate victims of terrible crimes.

It was May 11th, a Saturday, the last time anyone remembered seeing Marilee alive. She had just left her job and headed to the Sumter Highway gas station in Richland County. It was the kind of place you would hope would be safe, located right across from a high school. There was a golf course and country club nearby.

There was also someone who wished to do her harm.

What exactly went down at the gas station is unclear. What is known is that the attacker forced Marilee into the trunk of his car and drove off to a wooded area. There, he raped her or attempted to, undressed her, and beat her with a blunt object believed to have been a flower vase or cemetery urn. He reportedly hit her with such force that her skull fractured. There, she was left for several days while her worried family began a search.

The attacker was not a sophisticated criminal. For one, he was messy. He left her clothing and her purse, which had just four dollars in bills, out in the open. Marilee's car, a 1971 Chevrolet, was found at the scene the following Wednesday. The discovery brought several police officers to the scene. Less than two thousand feet from the vehicle and only ninety feet from the nearest road was what, or rather who, they were looking for.

The teenager was found wearing only her socks. Even after four days of exposure to the elements, a few things could still be gleaned about what had occurred, the most obvious being that Marilee had been the victim of a violent attack, but the signs of her resistance were also apparent. She had fought back.

Nobody could be linked to the killing during its immediate aftermath, and, with Shari's abduction taking place less than a month later, the theory that both crimes could have been committed by the same individual worried law enforcement—and the community. The fear that they or someone they knew could be next ran deep.

Early June only brought more troubling news. A college student attending the University of South Carolina had been taken to Charleston, though she was quickly released unharmed.

In the town of Irmo, a teenager was attacked by an intruder, and managed to fight them off. As summer came, tensions only rose with the heat.

Children who had expected to enjoy the warm weather outside found themselves disappointed as their frightened parents kept them indoors. "My mom took my car away from me," expressed Amy Bowen, a frustrated local teen. "She won't let me go anywhere. I have to stay home."

Residents could not stop looking over their shoulder, always on high alert for anyone who seemed suspicious. Unfortunately for some men, "suspicious" here meant simply having a closely-cropped beard like Shari's abductor was believed to have. It was not unheard of for men who fit this description to be stopped and questioned by law enforcement. It was the kind of paranoia that could have easily turned deadly, especially given the sudden rise of business at The Ballistics Center in Colombia by the middle of June. Karl Gowan, co-owner of the Center, was quoted in The State's June 24th issue: "We've got husbands buying guns for their wives, bringing children in and teaching them to shoot."

Marilee's murder was eventually tied to someone she knew: a seventeen-year-old coworker named James Donald Fossick, who was also thought to have possibly been her friend. Witnesses were able to confirm how and where Fossick had spent the day, except incredibly for one unaccounted hour—the hour it is believed Marilee's life was taken. Though Fossick confessed to the crime, he retracted his statement during the trial the following year, claiming it was actually Shane Parker, one of the witnesses, who was guilty.

It was a shock to many to discover that the perpetrator of this brutal killing was not only another teenager, but one who appeared to have no prior criminal record. There were doubts about Fossick's guilt from the start, including from his and Marilee's employer, Dr. Kauric, but not enough for a jury to find him innocent in January of 1986. It would later be revealed that, in 1984, Fossick had taken fourteen-year-old Robin Rose, forced her into the trunk at gunpoint, and drove her down the same dirt road where he would later take Marilee. However, the younger girl lived to tell the tale, though it was determined to be too much for jurors to hear.

Fossick was sentenced to life in prison, appealed ten years after the crime, in 1995, and was sentenced to life a second time. He remains in prison to this day.

It was a relief to the Whitten family to have their daughter's killer off the streets, but now that it was determined that Marilee and Shari's cases were unrelated due to the more personal nature of the former, and that revealed something about the world that shattered the community's innocence forever: there was not just one evil person running around free. Who knew how many there were? Anybody could become a victim, but anybody—including the people they thought they knew—could also be a murderer.

VII

The Request

It was difficult not to lose hope. Given the severity of Shari's medical condition, as well as the fact that her captor was refusing to allow them any direct contact with her, the Smith family was quickly reaching their emotional limits. Bob and Hilda, understandably, could not bring themselves to rest when the status of their daughter was still unknown. Their anxiety and sleep deprivation became so severe that a family doctor prescribed them both sleeping pills.

It had only been a few days, but fear made those days seem like they stretched on forever.

The community of Lexington County was still eager to assist in the search. A local print shop printed more than ten thousand missing person posters that were then distributed by volunteers all across the area. Lexington State Bank generously contributed five thousand dollars to a reward fund, but it was the individual contributions from individual private citizens that raised the fund up to an impressive twenty-five thousand dollars.

Sheriff Metts, for his part, was doing his best to keep positive about the search, and on June 4th, at a news conference outside the Smith family home, he announced that the search would be expanding beyond Lexington to Saluda County. Media outreach was proving helpful so far, at least in the sense that it was getting a reaction out of their suspect, though they still needed to be careful. "Because of the delicacy of the case at this time, I can't go into specifics on the information that has directed our search there."

Some of that information involved possible sightings of Shari alive and well in Saluda.

"I'm not going to give up," Metts continued. "Until I get something to make me believe there is no reason to keep searching. Our leads suggest that Shari is alive, and someone is holding her."

The Smith family themselves would go on to make another television appearance. "Shari, we love you so much," said Hilda to the cameras. "We're just not going to give up on finding you."

"We're not a family without you," Dawn added.

Again, theirs was a message for the suspect as much as it was a message for Shari. This sort of indirect communication was something that special agent John Douglas had experience with. In his book, Douglas writes: "I realized at that point that media was a two-way street. If we could determine that an UNSUB (unidentified suspect of an investigation) was following news accounts, we could publicize facts to get him to react in a certain way. That ultimately helped us catch and prosecute Wayne B. Williams for some of the Atlanta murders."

Douglas is, of course, referring to a series of murders, suspected to have been up to thirty, that occurred in Atlanta, Georgia, from 1979 to 1981. Out of those thirty victims, twenty-eight of them were children, with twenty-four deaths believed to have been caused by a man named Wayne Bertram Williams.

The idea to use media and news reports to their advantage came to detectives after receiving calls from someone claiming to be the real killer. The caller, who used racial slurs, told police he was going to strike again. He even told them where to find the next body along Sigmon Road. Douglas got the impression that their caller liked the idea of being in control and was reveling in the details of the crimes. There was one major issue with pursuing this lead; however, police were certain that this was not their man.

Police showed up at Sigmon Road, anyway, pretending to search for a body they knew was not there on the opposite side the imposter had told them to look for. This was intentional; they knew this kind of person would not waste an opportunity to call again to rub the supposed mistake in their faces—and he did, leading to his arrest.

The imposter, an older white male, was not a murderer, just a nuisance distracting from the real investigation. Still, it is likely his stunt inspired the real killer, Williams, into dumping the next body along Sigmon Road.

Speaking of serial killers, Douglas was getting the eerie feeling that they could possibly be dealing with another one. Having interviewed murderers in the past, he knew how they acted in the time before they were caught. Communicating with law enforcement as well as the families of their victims was not uncommon as evidenced by the actions of infamous criminals such Dennis Radar ("Bind Torture Kill") and the forever-elusive Zodiac Killer. These were people who liked taunting others and being in control more than anything.

What the Smith family were being forced to endure with these phone calls, however, felt particularly deranged.

As suspected, the Smiths got another call that same evening on June 4th, at around fifteen minutes before ten o'clock.

This time Dawn answered.

"Dawn?" asked the suspect.

"Yes."

"This is Shari Faye's request. Have your mother get on the other phone quickly."

"To get on the other phone," Dawn repeated. She was then heard calling out to Hilda.

"Get a pencil and paper ready," he instructed.

"Get a pencil and paper ready," said Dawn. "Okay."

"Okay."

"She's not on the phone yet."

"Well, I'll tell you this."

"Okay?"

"You are aware that was in Shari's own handwriting?"

"Yes, I am. All right?"

"Okay, now this is Shari's own words."

"Okay."

"So listen carefully. Say nothing unless you're asked."

"Okay."

"Okay, and it's not necessary… I know these calls are taped." He paused.

"Uh-huh."

"…and traced, but that's irrelevant now. There's no money demanded, so here's Shari Faye's last request. On the fifth day to put the family at rest, Shari Faye being freed. Remember, we are one soul now. When you locate... when located, you'll locate both of us together. We are one. God has chosen us. Respect all past and present requests. Actual events and times... jot this down. Hurry."

"All right. I'm doing it," Dawn replied.

"3:28 in the afternoon, Friday, 31st of May, Shari—"

"Wait a minute. Too fast. 3:28 afternoon..."

"Shari Faye was kidnapped by your mailbox with a gun. She had the fear of God in her, and she was at the mailbox. That is why she did not return back to her car."

"She had... she had to fear what?"

"Fear of God," he reiterated.

"Fear of God."

"Okay, 4:58 AM... no, I'm sorry. Hold on a minute. 3:10 AM. Saturday, the first of June, uh, she hand wrote what you received. 4:58 AM, Saturday, the... the first of June."

"Okay, Saturday, 1st of June, 4:58 AM."

"Became one soul."

"Became one soul," Dawn repeated.

On the other line, Hilda could be heard asking, "What does that mean?"

"No questions now," said the suspect.

"All right."

"Last, between four and seven Wednesday, tomorrow, have an ambulance ready. Remember, no circus."

"Four and…?"

"Prayer."

"Wait," Dawn asked. "Four and seven AM?"

"Four and seven in the afternoon, tomorrow," he clarified.

"In the afternoon."

"Tomorrow."

"Okay."

"Okay," he said. "Have an ambulance ready. Remember her request. No circus."

Dawn agreed.

The suspect went on, saying, "Prayers and relief coming soon. Please learn to enjoy life. Forgive. God protects the chosen. Shari Faye's important request. Rest tonight and tomorrow. Good shall come out of this. And please tell Sheriff Metts, search no more. Blessings are near. Tomorrow, Wednesday, four… four in the afternoon until seven in the evening. Ambulance ready. No circus.

"No circus. What does that mean?" Dawn tried to ask, but he ignored the question.

"You will receive last instructions where to find us. Please forgive—"

Hilda broke in. "Do not kill my daughter, please. I mean, please. Let me—"

"We love and miss y'all," the suspect interrupted. "Get good rest tonight."

"Listen—" Hilda pleaded.

"Goodbye."

"Wait a minute!"

"He's gone, mama," said Dawn. There was only silence on the other end.

VIII

The Discovery

WEDNESDAY, JUNE 5, 1985.

It had now been five days since Shari was abducted in front of her home, since the Smith family's lives were turned upside down. After so much time had been spent in the endless haze of worry, the four of them were exhausted. But at last, it would all be over soon.

The suspect had made some big proclamations during his last call. He claimed that Shari made requests, that Shari was still trying to communicate with them, albeit through her captor. She wanted an ambulance to be present at the scene and she did not want a media circus. The Smith family could not help but hang on to every word, and the suspect knew it. Dawn had been awake in her bed all night, her mind focused on her little sister.

How scared she must have been, how sick she must be feeling now. In an effort to put her mind at ease, she told herself that Shari was alive, that she would be coming home soon. She needed so badly to believe it because the other possibility was too dreadful to consider. Dawn knew that their mother felt similarly; Hilda rose to pack a bag containing her nightgown and toiletries to take with her to the hospital where she grew certain she would spend the night with Shari to keep her company after her ordeal.

They had to remain positive, but a sense of dread hung over. It was a feeling detectives could not quite shake as they made the necessary preparations to catch their man. Their plan? Get to the payphone before the suspect could. This required them to shut off a number of the payphones in the area; thereby limiting the number of places the suspect could make calls from, making him much easier to corner. Police would be ready and waiting for him, hiding out near the functioning phones.

Still, for now, they were stuck. Until the suspect made his next move, who knew which area they would be working in?

Another night in a series of agonizing, sleepless nights gave way to morning. Fear and hope rose with the summer sun. Finally, just before noon, they got the call they had been waiting for. Hilda answered.

On the other end, the suspect's voice was rushed, almost breathless as he spoke: "Listen carefully. Take Highway 378 west to the traffic circle. Take Prosperity exit, go one and a half miles, turn right at the sign Moose Lodge Number 103, then go one quarter mile, turn left at the white framed building, go back a yard, six feet beyond we're waiting. God chose us."

In a frustrating turn, it turned out the suspect had decided to call less than twenty minutes before the payphones had been scheduled to turn off. There was no way the suspect could have known that; it was just a bit of bad luck—a premonition, perhaps, of the worst that was still to come.

At least, that seemed to be what law enforcement was thinking when they moved out to the scene.

Hilda, understandably desperate to see her daughter, begged to go with Sheriff Metts and Police Captain Leon Gasque, but they had to leave her, as well as the rest of the Smith family, at home. Perhaps it seemed heartless of them at the moment, but it was for the best.

It would have simply been too dangerous to bring a civilian, especially one as close to the case as an immediate family member, to show up with police at an active crime scene. Not only was it dangerous—the suspect could very well be present and armed—but any interference at this point could seriously damage the investigation.

The main reason, of course, went unsaid: law enforcement did not want the Smith family to see what they were expecting to find.

The South Carolina Wilderness and Marine Resources Department sent out a helicopter while SLED officers and local cops rushed towards the scene. The Masonic Moose Lodge was located about sixteen miles from the spot where Shari had been abducted. It was a dour-looking, plain white building that stood out against the woods surrounding it. An aerial photograph of the scene shows several police vehicles converging on one side of it, while patches of bushes and trees stretched on towards the others.

Meanwhile, the Smith family huddled together in Dawn's bedroom. The knowledge that their lives were already forever changed weighed heavy on their hearts. The knowledge that the end was nearly here left them too distraught to speak. All they could do was wait and hold hands, praying silently for a miracle.

Less than forty minutes after the call, the helicopter picked up on something suspicious within the foliage below. It turned out the suspect had been meticulous in his directions. What they were looking for was almost exactly where he said it would be.

Fifty feet behind the lodge, six to eight feet beyond the tree line was Shari.

She was no longer alive.

IX

The End of the Search

IT IS NEVER EASY TO DELIVER BAD NEWS, IT WAS especially difficult for law enforcement in this case; in the few days they had spent in such close proximity to the Smith family, they had come to know them well. After so much waiting, so much terror, the worst had come true. Despite their best efforts, they had failed.

It was Police Captain Leon Gasque who faced the unenviable task of informing the family. He drove back to the Smith home and pulled up to their lengthy driveway. He could not help but move slowly, as though he were weighed down by the gravity of his terrible message. A distance of seven hundred feet separated him from their front door, but he would turn out to not need to cross the entire path, because Dawn had been waiting for him.

The moment she heard footsteps, she hurried outside. She met Gasque at the front steps. He looked at her; in that moment, he could not bring himself to say a word. Tears filled his eyes.

Dawn's heart sank. Inside, she was screaming. "And I just remember just having this fear of, oh my gosh, oh no!" she would later recall. Like Gasque, she too was in too much shock to speak.

The exact details of the meeting between Gasque and the Smiths are hazy. Emotions were running high, who could be bothered to keep a record of what was said as a family's life fell apart forever in an instant? Dawn felt sick. Gasque could not speak without choking up. Who knew what Bob and Hilda were feeling? It was like some horrible nightmare they could never wake up from.

"I'm so sorry," Gasque finally managed to say. "It is Shari, and she's dead. We found her body behind the Masonic Lodge."

Dawn recalled her mother letting out a wail.

"Are you sure it's Shari?" Bob asked. There was still a part of him that was in total disbelief.

"No," the captain replied sadly. "It's her."

"Not my baby! Oh god, not my baby!" Hilda sobbed. Her husband held her while he and Robert cried silently.

Then Dawn said something that shocked the captain. "Where is she? I want to see Shari for myself."

"No," Captain Gasque replied firmly. "I cannot let you do that."

"Why not?"

"It's not necessary for any family members to identify the body. It's in bad shape," he explained. "But we are sure it is Shari we found."

An uncomfortable quiet hung in the room. What more could be said? All Gasque knew was that he was no longer needed there. "I'm so, so sorry," he said. "I'm going to leave you alone now."

He was gone, and the four remaining members of the Smith family were, for the first time since the nightmare began, alone in their house together. They all sat in Dawn's bedroom and cried for a long, long time.

The Smith family were devout Christians, and though they never lost their faith, the pain of losing Shari was enough to shake her older sister to her core. In her memoir *Grace So Amazing*, Dawn recalls, "God, how could You? Why would You let this happen to us? How could You let Shari suffer? Oh, God, how much she must have suffered! Did You even listen to my constant prayers all this time? Didn't You hear anything I said? Evidently not! You could have stopped this from happening, couldn't You? Thanks a lot, God, for nothing."

Dawn's request to see her sister's body immediately following the news might seem strange. If there is one way that you hope to never see a loved one, it is as a corpse. But what she needed was closure; how else could she get past the knowledge that she would never see her little sister again?

Unfortunately for the Smith family, getting closure, if it were even possible, was still a long way away. The biggest obstacle was that there were still so many unanswered questions. The most obvious: who was responsible for her murder?

Law enforcement certainly had their work cut out for them. Their plans had already been complicated when the suspect beat them to the payphones before the scheduled shut down. This last phone call had been traced to a switch station on Camden Highway, and like all of the previous occasions, the suspect had been slick enough to leave no evidence behind.

Police knew they had been dealing with a calculating criminal, but they had no idea they were now hunting down someone so utterly depraved. They had seen this behavior before in only the most dangerous killers.

After taking Shari, the cruelest thing the suspect had done was give the Smith family false hope. He had essentially strung them along, forcing them to play some sick game that only he knew the rules to. This was the kind of person who revels in the suffering of their fellow human beings.

All this talk about returning Shari, being worried about her life, and the emotional wellbeing of her family—it was all an act.

The truth was that, aside from her letter, it had been impossible for Shari to try and communicate with anyone because she had been dead the whole time.

Constructing a timeline of events would prove tricky. Shari had been found wearing the same clothes she wore to her friend's pool party—the clothes she was last seen in: white shorts, a pair of black and yellow bikini bottoms, a yellow tank top, and a black-and-white striped blouse worn as a coverup. She was barefoot as she had left her shoes in her car. She still had the gold chain necklace around her neck her boyfriend Richard had gifted her. The only thing missing was one of her gold stud earrings.

Shari had been found lying on her back among the grass. Flies and other insects swarmed her. The sweltering heat contributed to the significant decomposition of her body, so much so that when Dr. Joel Sexton, a forensic pathologist at the Newberry Memorial Hospital, arrived at the scene, he could already tell that determining the exact cause of death would be difficult. Despite this, it was clear that Shari had not died here.

She had been dragged there. Detectives could make out a path running through a patch of broken bushes and plants. The killer must have brought her over to the back of the lodge in his vehicle and dragged her towards the woods, perhaps even that suspicious one Mrs. Butler had reported seeing—or maybe he was too smart for that and already got himself another car.

There were so many questions, and investigators had to work fast if they wanted any of those answers. For now, however, they would have to start with the most gruesome part of the work: forensics.

Much of the day had been spent photographing the area. The new people brought to the case, such as Dr. Sexton, were brought up to speed on the investigation, even getting copies of Shari's Last Will and Testament. Work at the crime scene lasted until six in the evening, after which Shari was transported to the Newberry Memorial Hospital.

Dr. Sexton performed the autopsy. One of the first things he and his team did was obtain Shari's dental records to compare. They were a perfect match; without a doubt, the body belonged to Shari. It was concluded that Shari, however she died, had not been beaten, shot, or stabbed. It could not be determined for certain if she had been sexually assaulted. The body was simply too decomposed to tell.

One important detail the pathologist was able to find were the ligature marks on her wrists. It seemed that, during the short time her captor kept her alive, she had been forced to spend it tied up with a rope. There was also the sticky residue of duct tape still on her face, meaning that her mouth or more of her face had been covered up.

Ultimately, it would be impossible to come up with a definitive cause of death, though there was no question as to whether she was murdered or not. As the hours went on, Dr. Sexton concluded that Shari had most likely been suffocated or strangled with "an instrument."

As far as the manner of death, he wrote, *since the death occurred during an abduction, the manner of death will still be homicide, regardless of whether it is due to depriving the decedent of water or from some type of homicidal asphyxia.*

This would be far from the only uncertainty that loomed over the minds of both the police and the public.

Sheriff Metts spoke at a news conference that Thursday. As hopeless as things were looking at the moment, he understood the importance of making it seem like law enforcement had the situation under control. They wanted to light a fire under their suspect, to make him nervous. It was one way to draw him out of hiding.

"We are concerned that this person may take his own life if he doesn't turn himself in," said Metts. "We don't want him to do that. I want to reassure him that we have no intentions of killing anyone. All we want to do is take this person into custody.

"We're trying to get this person to surrender. He needs help, and we want him to get it… He sounds as if he is afraid; as if he doesn't know whether to take his own life or turn himself in."

Special agent John Douglas had some serious doubts about the possibility that the suspect might harm himself. After all, given the lies and false hope he had given the Smiths over the phone, everyone knew he was all talk—Douglas had dealt with enough criminals to know that. Still, it was not an impossibility. If there was even the slightest chance that the suspect was remorseful, they had to take it.

Despite his words, Sheriff Metts did not have high hopes. It was a precarious balancing act to appear both merciful and intimidating. "If he's having fun jerking us around, he can continue. The investigation is going full blast and we are not stopping until we catch him, I promise!"

The plan seemed to work, because later that day, the suspect made another phone call.

X

The Calls Continue

"*THIS IS CONCERNING SHARI FAYE SMITH. I want to use you as a medium. Can you handle it?*"

It was Thursday, June 6th—the day after the discovery of Shari's body. After the speech given by Sheriff Metts at the news conference, nobody knew what to expect from the suspect. Police certainly did not anticipate that his next phone call would be made to an unrelated person. At around two thirty that afternoon, Charlie Keyes, an investigative reporter for WIS-TV, the local news station in Colombia, answered the phone.

Keyes accepted the opportunity to be used as a medium between the suspect and law enforcement.

"Okay, now listen carefully," continued the suspect. "I can't live with myself, Charlie, and I need to turn myself in, and I'm afraid–and you're a very intelligent person, and I want you to be there with Sheriff Metts and all the officers he wants at his home in the morning, and you answer the phone."

"At whose home?" Keyes asked.

"At Sheriff Metts home. Hurry now. Don't answer any questions unless I ask. You be there and answer the phone."

The suspect then gave the following instructions: Charlie Keyes, who typically appeared on the television news at seven in the evenings, was to film that day's segment at Sheriff Mett's house. He demanded that "Shari Faye's priest" from the Lexington Baptist Church also be in attendance.

Keyes was told that he would have to set the plan in motion the second after this call, as to not waste any precious time. When calling, Keyes was to recite details from Shari's Will and Testament (which, at this point, had not yet been released to the public) to prove that he was the real deal.

If Keyes did exactly as he was told, the suspect promised to give him an exclusive interview.

But the suspect was not done talking just yet.

"Now, Charlie... please... it just went bad. I know her family and he, and well, I just made a mistake. It went too far. All I wanted to do was make love to her," the suspect confessed. "I didn't know she had the rare disease, and it just got out of hand. I got scared and I–I have to do the right thing, Charlie... now please, work with me, because I feel like I can trust you, and I've listened to you many times. That's why I picked you as the medium."

Charlie Keyes played along. It was vital to keep the suspect speaking. Everything he said was being recorded by the television station, as was the standard procedure for all the phone calls they received. The tape was to be sent to law enforcement.

"Please forgive me!" cried the suspect. "God forgive me and take care of me. I need the help bad, and I want to do the right thing, and tell them to please honor Shari Faye's request: casket closed. Plus, take her hands and fold them on her stomach, like she's praying. You understand that?"

Finally, the call ended. The tape was handed over to law enforcement, who immediately noticed some strange things about it, namely, the suspect's insistence that he knew the Smiths personally. In his book, Douglas writes:

"His statement: *'I didn't know she had the rare disease'* proved we were right when we assessed the business about his being a friend of the family, which he also said in calls with Hilda and Dawn, as bunk. Anyone truly close to the family knew of Shari's condition. It was just another part of his fantasy, trying to draw a connection with this beautiful girl he had first seen at a distance. We also knew, despite his protestations, that he was not going to turn himself in. He was getting too much satisfaction out of this. The only true words he uttered in the entire exchange with the reporter were when he said he'd wanted *'to make love to her.'* But whether he was able to accomplish that as a sexual assault while she lived or not, he would have known he would have to kill her afterward… Did he actually feel guilty about what he had done to Shari? Perhaps there might have been a tinge of guilt, though even that I doubted. What we firmly believed from his signature and M.O. (modus *operandi) was that if this individual was not caught, and caught soon, he would kill again."*

These were foreboding words, and unfortunately, Douglas's suspicions would not prove to be unfounded.

Meanwhile, if life for the Smith family was not difficult enough given the tragedy they faced, the suspect, as he was wont to do, had to come back and make things even worse.

Later that same day, Dawn had taken the family dog, Lady, out for some fresh air after returning from some painful but necessary errands. What should have been a simple, every day task for most people became stressful with the knowledge that Shari's killer was still out there. The Smith house was in clear view of the woods, and who knew who could be hiding in there? It was risky leaving the house by herself, but Dawn desperately needed to be alone for a bit.

In the kitchen, Beverly, Dawn's aunt and Bob's sister, heard the phone ring. "Hello?"

"I have a collect call for Dawn Smith," said the phone operator.

"Dawn is not taking any calls," said Beverly. "Can I have a name, please?"

"Please put Dawn on the line." This was a different voice; it was a man's. The Smiths might have recognized it as belonging to the suspect, but Beverly was unfamiliar with it.

"Dawn can't come to the phone right now. This is her Aunt Beverly."

The man on the other end seemed annoyed. "Well, may I speak to Mrs. Smith? This is an emergency."

"Well, I'm sorry, she is being sedated and cannot come to the phone. She's asleep."

"Okay. May I speak to Bob Smith?" he asked.

"Bob has Dawn up to the funeral home. You realize the situation with their daughter. Wait one moment. You… you asked to speak with Mrs. Smith?"

"Or Dawn. I'd rather speak to Dawn."

"To Dawn?" Beverly repeated.

"Uh-huh."

"Uh, well..." Beverly hesitated. Just what kind of person was she dealing with here? "Let me see if we can find her."

"Okay. Hurry up."

"All right. They're looking right now."

The operator was still on the line. "Thank you, ma'am."

"Okay, thank you, operator," said the man. "I'll speak to anybody that comes to the phone now."

"This is her Aunt Beverly."

The operator cut in again. "Collect from Joe Wilson. Will you accept the charge?"

"Yes, we'll accept the charge," she said. "This is Shari's Aunt Beverly. I'll be happy to speak to you. Who am I speaking to, please?"

"I want to speak to Dawn," he insisted.

"We're trying to locate her. In the meantime, I'll be happy to help you."

"No, thank you. I'll have to go then if I can't talk to her."

"She's coming," Beverly replied. "They're looking for her immediately. Just one moment, they're... they're trying to find her. She..."

The man was ready to end the call. "Okay, operator—"

"Wait one moment, please! She had walked outside to walk the dog. They are looking for her."

"Operator," said the man, ignoring Beverly's pleas. "Is the operator on the line?"

Outside, Dawn did not get the chance to enjoy her solitude, however. Bob had noticed her absence and became worried. "Dawn!" he shouted, loud enough to startle his daughter. "Dawn! Where are you?"

Dawn sensed a tinge of anger in his voice, so she returned quickly, entering through the basement and making her way up to the kitchen. "Here I am," she replied.

"What were you doing? Where were you?" he asked, frantic. "Don't you know better than to go outside without telling anyone? Get the phone!"

Dawn felt her heart drop. She already knew who it was. Her Aunt Beverly had the phone and looked nervous.

"Here's Dawn right now," she said, handing her niece the receiver.

[The following section of this book is an attempt to reconstruct as much of the ensuing conversation as possible, pieced together from publicly available information from various sources.]

"Hello?" Dawn struggled to say. She was still out of breath from a combination of rushing inside and anxiety.

"Dawn?" There was that loathsome voice, though there was something markedly different about it this time. He stopped trying to disguise his voice, meaning he was becoming bolder.

"Yes."

"I'm calling for Shari Faye," he said. "And are you aware that I'm turning myself in tomorrow morning?"

"No."

"Well, have you talked to Sheriff Metts or Charlie Keyes?"

This confused Dawn. Who was Charlie Keyes? The name was familiar, but she struggled to recall who it belonged to, and when she remembered Keyes was a newscaster, she only felt more lost. "Uh, no."

"Well, talk to them and listen carefully."

Dawn was struggling to keep her composure. This man had done the unthinkable to her family, and here he was telling her what to do. It made her feel sick. She choked down her rage and managed to utter a tense, "Okay."

"I have to tell you this, that uh, Shari asked me to uh, turn myself in on the… after the fifth day after they found her."

"Wait," said Dawn. She reached for something to write with. "I'm trying to write this down."

"Don't write it down," he said.

"Don't write it down?"

"Don't write it down," he reiterated.

"Okay," Dawn replied, though she had no intention of following his order. Taking notes during these phone calls was important, especially if there were any problems with the recorder.

The suspect went on. "And uh, or get myself straight with God and uh, turn myself completely over to Him, so I have to turn myself over to Him."

"Okay."

"And uh, they'll… uh, Charlie Keyes… you'll know what I'm talking about when you talk to him. He will not be able to get a personal interview with me in the morning. I'm uh, there'll be a letter. It's already been mailed. An exact copy for you and for him and it's… with pictures."

"A copy to me?"

"Yes, and him at his home of pictures of Shari Faye from the time… even… I made her stand up to her car and took two pictures and all through the thing, and the letter will describe exactly what happened from the time I picked her up until the time uh, I called and told y'all where to find her."

"Okay," Dawn replied. She hoped he could not hear her scribbling away.

"And I'll be doing the same thing in the morning at 6 AM, and tell the sheriff and Charlie Keyes... Charlie Keyes, I used him as a medium today and I talked to him."

"Okay, 6 AM. What will you be doing in the morning?" Dawn asked.

"Well, he'll know."

He'll know? What did that mean? "Oh, he'll—"

The suspect cut her off. "He'll already know."

"He'll know," Dawn repeated, fighting the urge to scream at him.

"Okay, and also that uh, uh, that I will be armed, but by the time they find me, I won't be dangerous."

"You... you..." Dawn could not find the right words. What did he mean by that? Was he really implying that he would take his own life?

"Do you understand that?" he asked.

"You will be armed..."

"But by the time they find me, I won't be dangerous."

"What does that mean?"

He was practically rambling now. "Well, I... Shari Faye said if I couldn't live with myself and she wouldn't forgive me if I didn't turn myself over and turn myself in or turn myself over to God. So I'm going to have to... I just... this thing got out of hand and all I wanted to do was make love to Dawn. I've been watching her for a couple of—"

Dawn was just as disgusted as she was afraid. She hoped she had heard him wrong. "To who?"

"To... I'm sorry, to Shari," he clarified. "And I watched her for a couple of weeks and uh, it just got out of hand and Dawn... Dawn, I hope you and your family forgive me for this."

This is what he was asking of her? After everything he had done to them, to Shari? He had a lot of nerve for even bringing the idea of forgiveness up. However, as much as she wanted to tell him off, she knew she had to keep him on the line. "You're not going to kill yourself, are you?"

"I... I don't... I can't live in prison and go to the electric chair. I can't do that. I... this is the only way I can get myself straight. I'm very sick and... but I... I can't go through—"

What did Dawn care if this horrible man killed himself? As far as she was concerned, the world would likely become a better place without him in it. "We don't want you to die," she said, unable to even feign sympathy. "We want to help you. Don't kill yourself."

"No, I just uh, you can't take someone's life, and this is the way it's going to have to be. Shari said—"

"Well, see, listen to me. Okay?" Dawn interrupted.

"Well, listen, I have to go—"

"No," she demanded. She was sick of him telling her to listen, to follow his commands. Now it was his turn to pay attention. "I've got to tell you something, okay? This is important."

"I know these calls—"

Don't let him change the subject, she thought. "God can—"

"—are being traced."

"God… well, that's okay. But God can forgive you and erase all of that."

"Dawn…" It sounded like his voice was breaking. Was he finally showing some real emotion? "I can't… I can't live with myself—"

"And we can forgive you, too," Dawn added, hoping that would keep him talking.

"—in prison for the rest of myself or go to the electric chair."

It was clear that he was getting so caught up in his own feelings that he was not even listening to her. That she had to console him now felt particularly cruel. "Listen," she spoke over his cries. "Shari's at peace with God. She's better off than any of us."

"Well, I want to say something to you that she told me."

"Okay." Dawn continued to write.

"Shari… oh boy… Shari Faye said that uh… she did not cry the entire time. She was very strong-willed and she said that uh, she did not want y'all to ruin your lives, and to go on with your lives like the letter said," he said. "And I've never lied to you before, right? Everything I've told you came true, right?"

"Yes," Dawn replied, though she felt unsure.

"Okay, so this is going to have to be the way it is and she said that uh, she wasn't scared; that she knew she was going to be an angel and if I took the latter choice that she suggested to me, that she would forgive me, but our God's going to be the major judgment and she'll probably end up seeing me in heaven, not in hell. And uh, she requests… now please, remember this. Now she requests that y'all be sure to take her hands and fold them in… on her stomach like she's praying—"

"Okay."

"…and that closed casket…"

"Yeah," said Dawn. She needed him to continue, as painful as it was. It took police time to trace calls. Maybe then they would finally get somewhere.

"They already made those plans?" he asked.

"Yes."

"Okay... and please have Charlie Keyes with Sheriff Metts, and Charlie knows what to do in the morning and have an ambulance and probably... before they get there, they might as well have a hearse also and uh, be at the traffic circle."

"The—"

"And I'm not in... I'll be... I'm just going to allow myself enough time to get in the area and get set up. I'm not in the area now. And uh, it'll be at 6 in the morning that I'll call his office, and by the time they reach me, I'll be... be straight with God and uh, Shari said please take the gold necklace that she had on and the... she had one earring on in her left ear..."

"Uh-huh."

"...and uh, save those things and treasure them."

"Save them?"

"Yes."

That was a bit of an odd request for Shari to have made. That necklace had been a gift from her boyfriend. She had been crazy about him, so why not leave him with something of hers to cherish? "She doesn't want Richard to have the necklace?"

"Uh, she said something... there was some special jewelry in her room that she said. I forgot what... it might have been the necklace. But uh, yeah, go... go ahead, but the rest of her stuff is irre... is irrelevant."

"Okay."

"She felt that y'all would divvy up. And—"

"What about her high school ring?" Dawn asked. That ring had not been found with Shari's body, which was unusual because she hardly ever took it off. It was also something Dawn knew her parents would want to have.

"Uh, that's... she said everything else would be decided by the family." The suspect sounded unsure, as though he were spinning the story right as they were speaking. Dawn worried he would get overwhelmed and hang up.

Dawn hoped that he was at least telling the truth about her sister's final moments. "But Shari was... was not afraid and she didn't cry or anything?"

"No," he said. "She didn't do anything. And uh, can you handle it if I tell you how she died?"

She paused. By now, Dawn was well aware that he did not actually care about her pain. She knew causing suffering was his goal. She tried not to let it show that she was hurting. "Okay."

"Okay, be strong now. She said she... you were. She told me all about the family and everything. We talked and... oh God. And I am a family friend. That's the sad part."

Dawn didn't believe that, either. "You are a family friend?"

"Yeah, and that's why I can't face y'all."

She thought she heard him trying not to laugh.

"You... you'll find out in the morning or tomorrow," he continued, though he was becoming less and less coherent. "But uh, forgive me and, uh, Dawn, uh, Shari... I don't know whether you were aware of..."

The transcript of the phone call takes a stop here. The full conversation, including the more details of the suspect's recollection of the crime, does not appear to have been released to the public. According to the February 15th issue of The State, "portions of the recording that some people might find objectionable" were omitted from publication. The following is where the recording continued.

"Okay," the suspect began. "I tied her up to the bedpost and uh, with electric cord. And I took duct tape and wrapped it all the way around her head and suffocated her and tell the coroner or get the information out how she died and uh, I was unaware she had this disease. I probably wouldn't ever taken her. Ah uh, I shouldn't have took her anyway. It got out of hand."

Dawn tried not to cry. It took all her strength to remain on the line with this monster. She could not understand how Sheriff Metts thought it was okay for her to have to listen to all this. "Uh-uh," was all she could say.

"And uh, I'd asked her out before, and she said she would if she wasn't going with anybody." Just another one of his sick fantasies. "Ah uh, she also said that uh… oh yeah, make sure Charlie Keyes… you know him? The reporter on WIS?"

"I can't think of who he is right now."

"Okay, they'll know who he is. He's the one who wears the bowtie on Channel 10. He's the head news fellow on this case for Channel 10. Tell him to be sure to get in touch with Ann David because—"

"Ann Davis?"

"Yeah. She's probably already told him some information. I had to use them for mediums because they were taping your house and stuff. And I know the ironic part… I had to see what was going on at the house… at your house," he clarified.

He came back to the house?

"Yes," said Dawn.

"And I was there Saturday morning for the search."

"You were there at the search Saturday?"

"Yes, I was. And if… oh God, Dawn. I wish, I wish y'all could help me, but it's just too late."

"Let me tell you something, okay? God can forgive you."

"Well, I have to go now, Dawn. I know—"

"—and through God, we can forgive you, also."

"Well, uh, Dawn… will you forgive me then?"

"Yes."

"Your family? But I... I just... it... it's... I'll have to take the other choice that–that Shari Faye said to me. I just can't live with myself like this. I'm not—"

"I think that you just need to think about that a little harder, that you—"

"I'm not going to be caged up like a dog. Okay, now, is there any other questions... short. I've got to do now. Time's running out."

"Uh, when... when you killed Shari, was she at peace? She wasn't afraid or anything?"

"She was not. She was at peace. She knew that God was with her and she was going to become an angel."

"And... and she wrote that letter to us of her own free will and all that was—"

"She sure did. Everything I've told y'all has been the truth. It... hasn't everything... everything came true?"

"Yes. It has."

"Okay, and now, I'll be in the area uh.... just a long enough time to set this up for myself..."

"Uh-huh."

"...and uh, like I said, I... also Charlie and everything requested, I mean, I told you that I requested Shari... I asked Shari Faye if I could do this and she said that it was fine with her to have the minister... the preacher from Lexington Baptist, be in the ambulance."

"Be in the ambulance. Lewis Abbott?" Dawn asked, recalling the name of their pastor.

"Huh?"

"Lewis Abbott?"

"Uh, yeah, I forgot. She... she told me his name. I forgot who it was. The who that was going to... y'all's regular minister with the church. That's him, okay?"

"Okay."

"The one that's going to do the funeral on Saturday?"

"Yes."

"Okay."

"Can… can I ask you one more question?"

"One more and that's it."

"When… when you uh, you told us that you… Shari was kidnapped at gunpoint?"

"Yeah."

"But she knew you?"

"Yeah. At first, see, I pulled up and uh, I'm telling you the truth. I have no reason to lie to y'all."

"Okay."

"I've always told you the truth, right?"

"Right."

"Okay, and uh, I had her–asked her to stand there and I took two instant pictures."

"You asked her to stand where?"

"At the mailbox with her car in the background. Those pictures... detailed pictures... will be with... with the letter you'll receive probably... since I'm out of town, probably not till Saturday."

"Uh-huh."

"And Charlie Keyes will get a copy and your family will get a copy and it's addressed to you unless the mail holds it up."

"So she didn't realize you were fixing to kidnap her?"

"That's exactly right."

"Okay."

"And uh, she's uh, she uh, what else? She doesn't uh... so I'll just be in there long enough to get set up for tomorrow morning and tell the.... Sheriff Metts that it's no use in uh... uh, trying to trace these calls or catch me. It's too late now. I won't be taken alive. And also, Dawn, that uh, uh, he can just call off the damn search. It's... it's over now. And—"

"Why are you talking?"

"I don't want people out there wasting their time and… and everything I've told you is true and this is coming true also. I just can't live with it. I can't take it anymore. Shari Faye was right. We… I feel like… I got close to her and we… she showed me things. She was very—" He cut himself off. "Oh, okay. Any more questions?"

"Uh, why are you talking to me instead of mom?"

"She felt like you were strong-willed, more than your mother."

"Oh, did you start talking to her?"

"Who?"

"Mother, at first."

"Yeah," he replied. "That was your mother."

"Oh, I was outside. I didn't know."

"Uh, she said it was your aunt, but it was your mother, correct?"

"Uh, no, that was my aunt that answered the phone," she clarified.

"Oh, it was? Okay. No, she said something about your mother being under medication. Shari told me... Shari Faye told me... remember that I told you on the fifth day to let them know where she was so her blessings of the body could be blessed, right?"

"Why on the fifth day did she want us to find her? Why not—"

"I don't know. She just... she just said that. I don't know. I don't have any idea. And uh, I'm telling you exactly how she died, so she died of suffocation. And so, you know, the... okay, anything else?"

"Why did... why did you do that?"

"She... I gave her a choice. I... to shoot her or give her a drug overdose or suffocate her."

All of the despair he had been showing was gone. Now he was sounding disturbingly nonchalant, as though he were talking about the most normal things in the world.

Dawn cried. "Why did you have to kill her?"

"It just got out of hand. I got scared because... uh, only God knows, Dawn. I don't know why. God forgive me for this. I hope and I got to straighten it out or he'll send me to hell and I'll be there the rest of my life, but I'm not going to be in prison and the electric chair."

"But I don't think taking your life is the answer to this. Or—"

"I'll... I'll think..."

"—or to forgive you."

"I'll think about it. Well, Dawn, I've got to go now. It's been too long and, ah, tell them to just forget about the search. I'll be in the area long enough in the morning for them to... ah, find me and by the time I call, ah, there, Charlie Keyes will know exactly the set-ups."

"Well—"

"I hope now, ah, I know I'm staying on the phone, all right, they are taping this. I don't want anything messed up, okay?"

"Okay,"

"They are taping it, right?"

"Uh-huh."

"Okay, good. Okay and anything else?"

"Uh, I, uh, just… ah…" There were countless things Dawn wanted to ask this man, but she could not string the words together. She was feeling exhausted.

"Oh, yeah, let me tell you. The other night they almost caught me." He laughed. "I wanted them to catch me. I felt that way all the time, but now—"

"When… when was this?"

"Ah, when I called you at 9:45."

"When you were over near Jake's Landing?"

"Yeah. I was at the Fast Fare thing. I pulled out twenty yards in front of two flashing lights—"

"What color car did you have?" Dawn asked.

"They hit it dead on it, red, and they didn't even, Dawn, I can't get over this. They didn't even turn around and follow me, and I cut right at that blinking light down there to go the back way on Old Cherokee Road." He laughed again. "And there was a highway patrolman or somebody in front of me and let me turn right on Old Cherokee Road. Can you believe it?"

"So you really wanted to be caught?"

"At that time, but it's too late now."

"What kind of car was it?"

"Oh, well, they were mighty close. I... Dawn... they're not going to catch me, and I... I can't give you much information because I got to make it back in time, and they'll stop me before I get back if I tell you, but they're right, it was a red one, and I almost got caught three or four times."

"Was it a red Jetta?" she asked, hoping she might get more out of him at this point.

"Dawn, that's irrelevant now. If I die now or if I die at six in the morning, it's irrelevant. Well, listen., ah, Dawn—"

"I really... I wish you would—"

"Anything else?" he spoke over her.

"I wish you would not kill yourself."

"And she told me to tell you, please go back to Carowinds. I know you live in Charlotte, and… ah, I know a lot about your family, and ah, go back and start singing and give it your best and that she knows that she'll be singing like crazy. She was, ah, when she said that, she was smiling. She'll be singing like crazy."

"She was smiling?"

"She was smiling, and, well—"

"So, she wasn't afraid the whole time?"

"No, never."

"Because she knew that she was going to be with God?"

"That's exactly right, the whole time. She's so strong-willed and, and—"

"But I just… really, I wish that you wouldn't think about killing yourself."

"I will, Dawn."

"You need to think about it a lot because—"

"Okay, well, put it this way. If I… if I decide between now and six in the morning, I'll, ah, oh, I'll—"

"Listen, our prayers will be for you."

"Okay. I'll call you collect."

"Did you hear what I said?" asked Dawn, growing irritated. "Will you be home tonight?"

"We… we are home tonight. Can I ask you… listen, our prayers will be with you, okay? God can do anything, and he can forgive you for this."

"Yeah, but you know what's going to happen to me, Dawn? I'm going to be fried."

"You don't know that," she said, trying her best to sound reassuring. "God can work miracles. You don't know that it'll happen to you—"

"Well, Dawn…"

"God is merciful no matter what we do."

"It's time now, it's time. I got to go now and I'll just… I'll think about it, but I've got a lot of things on my mind now. I know you know that, right?"

"Right."

"And, ah, ah… you answer the phone every time it rings tonight."

"Me answer the phone every time it rings?"

"That's right and if it's collect… and I'll say from the break of day, you'll know."

"If we're asleep, you let it keep ringing, okay?"

"I will, I will. God bless all of us."

"God bless you too."

"And—"

By now, Hilda had woken up from her sedated sleep. She had heard Dawn talking for a long time and wanted to give this man a piece of her mind. She reached out for the receiver. "Wait, mother wants to say something to you."

"Please—"

"Listen," she said. "Mom wants to say something to you."

"All right. Just one thing and then I'm gone," he replied, sounding nervous.

"Hello?" said Hilda.

"Yes."

"Well, hurry," he demanded. "Just say one thing and that's it. Dawn will tell you and you listen to the recordings, and there will be a letter you'll receive probably the next day with pictures and detailed information from the time I picked Shari up at the mailbox until tonight and my departure from the earth. It's over. I will not be taken alive. Dawn told me to turn myself in or turn myself over to God or I'll never live in peace and never be forgiven and go to heaven."

"Well," Hilda began. "Turn yourself over to God. That's most important."

"I am and this is the only way. I'm not going to spend my life in prison and go to the electric chair." His voice was breaking again.

"Ah—"

"Well, ah, Dawn knows everything and, ah, God bless all of us and I hope—"

"Listen, I want to ask you something."

He seemed to already know what she wanted to ask. "This just got out of hand…"

"All you had to do was let her go."

"I was scared. She… she… she was dehydrating so bad."

Hilda could not hold back her tears. "You could have called me for medicine. I would have met you anywhere."

"Well, that's irrelevant now," he replied coldly.

"Oh. I mean all you had to do was let her go. Such a beautiful young life."

"I know that. That's why I have to join her now, hopefully, and, ah, Mrs. Smith, please, ah, please, uh… uh, okay. Well, that's it. I got to go."

"Did she know you when you stopped her?"

"Yeah, ah, there'll be pictures and I took pic… two pictures Instamatic of… I made her stand… well, before she knew I was going to kidnap her, I asked her to stand at the mailbox and you'll see her picture, her car door, and cars in the background, and, ah, there will be pictures all, I think there's about eight pictures and Charlie Keyes will be receiving a set and a detailed letter, like I told you, at his house, and I… if it's… if the mail doesn't slow it down, which it probably will, if you don't get it tomorrow, you'll get it the next day. You'll get exact copies, the pictures that he gets and, ah, exact letters, too."

He barely made sense. A different approach was necessary. "Did you know all of us or just Shari?" Hilda asked.

"I know the whole family, unfortunately," he replied. "That's why I can't face you. Okay, well, Mrs. Smith, please, ah, if I decide different, I've already told Dawn what's going to happen. Her answer the phone tonight only and it will be collect and I'm going to allow myself enough time to get back to the area to set everything up if you don't hear from me tonight, and Sheriff Metts and Charlie Keyes… I used him as a medium today because I knew the calls were being traced, and they came real close to catching me three or four different times and they were correct… I am in a red vehicle."

"What kind?"

"I'm sorry, I don't want them to catch me before I meet my Maker on judgment day."

Anger rose in Hilda. "You think the Maker's going to forgive you now?"

"He'll... He'll do that or I'll be crucified and go to hell."

"That's right," she agreed.

"Well—"

"And you need to meet somebody who can talk to you," she said, forcing her tone to sound softer.

"Well, I'm... I've got a lot to think about and I'm... I'm gone, Mrs. Smith, and, ah, please. I—" He was stuttering now, bordering on hysterics. How could he change moods so fast? "I know this might be selfish, but, ah, you all please, ask a special prayer for me? Your... your daughter said that she was not afraid and she was strong-willed. She, ah, knew that she was going to heaven, was going to be an angel, and like I told Dawn, she was going to be singing like crazy, and—"

"Did she—"

"When she said that, she was smiling," he said. He almost sounded like he was trying to be kind.

"Did you tell her you were going to kill her?"

"Yes, I did and I gave her a choice, like, it's on the recording. I asked her if she wanted to be drug overdosed, shot, or... ah, suffocated, and she picked suffocation."

"My God, how could you?" asked Hilda, fully sobbing.

"Well, forgive us. God… God…"

"Not us," she clarified. "You."

"God only knows why this happened. I don't know," he said, clearly getting tired himself. "It just got out of hand."

"That's… I thought… you know what?"

"Good bye, Mrs. Smith."

"I thought you were considerate and loving and a kind person," she cried, but there was no longer another person at the end of the line to hear her. He had already hung up.

This lengthy phone call was traced to a phone booth at the Grand Central Truck Stop at I-77 and Highway 200, located in Great Falls, South Carolina. Like all the previous times, he left no trace.

XI

The Funeral

I WILL NEVER BE IN MY SISTER'S WEDDING, *crying joyfully as she walks down the aisle in her flowing gown. Instead, I'll cry tears of anguish at her funeral.*

These thoughts weighed heavily on Dawn's mind as she helped her parents plan Shari's funeral. Together, they decided that Shari would be buried in a silver coffin. The flowers set on top would be pink roses. After the sad news of Shari's death, touches of pink, Shari's favorite color, could suddenly be found all over Lexington, mainly in the form of ribbons attached to mailboxes or bumper stickers. The movement was called the Pink

Ribbon Crusade—the initials PRC also stood for "People Really Care."

Other residents wanted a more direct way to help out. Robert Gillespie, a store clerk, told *The Charlotte Observer*, "Just about everybody says that if they caught (Smith's killer) before the police, it would be their pleasure to save the state the electricity expense."

All that noise the suspect made about the family honoring Shari's request turned out to have been pointless. Shari's body was in such bad shape that having an open casket was simply not an option. Shari would not even be dressed; her mother could only lay her blue homecoming dress over the body.

The funeral service was held at the Lexington Baptist Church, during which Dawn spent looking downwards, avoiding the gazes of other people. Her emotions were running high, fluctuating between despair and numbness. She could only imagine the kind of pain her parents were enduring.

The church was packed, evidence of the impact this terrible crime had on the community. The funeral had been scheduled for the Saturday after Shari's classmates returned from their graduation cruise, the trip she had so looked forward to, so that all her friends could be in attendance. Dawn would later estimate that there had to have been at least one thousand people there that day.

Among the massive crowd were a number of SLED agents. They were there not only to support the Smith family, who they had grown close to during the past few days, but out of necessity. It is not unheard of for murderers to attend the memorials of their victims or visit their graves, sometimes as a way to relive the "high" of their crimes. A man as sick and twisted as Shari's killer certainly seemed like the type to twist the knife in a family's emotional wounds. Both Dawn and Hilda had been instructed not to go out unless they were accompanied by an officer.

It was a possibility that Dawn was well aware of. As the funeral progressed and mourners came up to her to offer their condolences, she grew paranoid that any of them could be her sister's killer. A white man with a close-cropped beard, receding hairline, and brown hair? There had to have been a million men in Columbia who fit that description. The man who took Shari's life could have been almost anyone among the crowd, hidden only by how unexceptional he looked, his ability to play the role of a normal man.

A scream interrupted her thoughts. A friend of Shari's had collapsed to the ground, kicking and screaming. She was terrified that the killer was coming to take her next. A ripple of fear ran through the crowd, causing several other women to cry out in fear.

Then a familiar voice cut through the chaos.

"Whoever is responsible for this, I believe you are here!" said a church friend. He held his arms up like a preacher as he spoke. "Come forward right now! There is no bitterness or hatred."

The man's impassioned cry was cut short. Sheriff Metts got the man into his patrol car while other officers led the Smith family away from the commotion.

This strange outburst was eventually attributed by someone Dawn knew personally, and she did not believe for a second that he was dangerous. Others were suspicious of this man, who was in his thirties and spent much of his time with the church youth group, but police found he had nothing to do with any crime. He was just an awkward family friend overcome by grief and emotion trying to help in the only way he could think of.

Who knows, Dawn later thought. He may have been right. The killer could have been there among them the entire time.

The family had just returned home when the phone rang. Dawn hurried to pick up the receiver, a feeling of dread forming in her stomach. "Hello?"

The operator spoke first. "I have a collect call for Dawn Smith from Shari. Will you pay for the call?"

"From who?" she asked, feeling outraged.

"Shari."

Dawn let out a long sigh. "Yes."

Now that terrible, familiar voice came through. "Dawn, like the break of day."

"What?"

"Like the break of day," he repeated. "Is this Dawn Smith?"

"Yes," she confirmed. "It is."

"Okay, you know this is not a hoax call, correct?"

"Yes."

"Did I catch you off guard?"

"Well, yeah," Dawn admitted. "Because they said it was from Shari."

"No, I said concerning Shari Faye. Everybody screwed up her—excuse my French. Okay? Now listen carefully." He was speaking plainly, sounding almost casual, as though they were old friends chatting. "Ah, Dawn. I'm real afraid now and everything and—"

Dawn wasn't buying this act again. "Uh-huh."

"And I have to, ah, make a decision. I'm going to stay in this area until God gives me the strength to decide which way… and I did go to the funeral today."

"You did?" Dawn asked, unable to hide her shock.

"Yes, and ah, that ignorant policeman… he even directed me into a parking space," said the suspect. "Fellow, blue uniform outside, and they were taking license plate numbers down and stuff. Please tell Sheriff Metts I'm not jerking anybody around. I'm not playing games, this is reality and I'm not an idiot. When he finds my background, he'll see that I'm a highly intelligent person."

Dawn stayed quiet—not that he seemed to notice.

"Okay, and I want to fill in some gaps here between now and next Saturday, the anniversary of Shari Faye…" The suspect paused for a moment. "I'm going to do one way or the other and if God gives me the strength before then, ever when and I'll call you and give you… all I'll say is—"

"Between now and next Saturday?" Dawn asked. That was a full week away, a strangely long time.

"Yes."

"I think you need to make a decision before then," she replied.

"Well, now listen carefully, don't ask questions. Think of questions you want but not now, okay… and I'll code so you know it won't be a hoax. I don't want… I never wanted that." Another pause. "Okay, we'll still use… when you answer the phone or whoever, I'll say, Dawn, like the break of day."

Dawn wrote everything down.

"We'll only know that, okay? All right, and, ah, I could tell her casket was closed, but did y'all honor her request for folding her hands?"

"Yes. Yes, we did, of course." Dawn struggled not to yell or cry at this point.

"Okay, she'll like that. That'll please her. Okay, and ah, tell Sheriff Metts, the FBI, damn, that's like the fear of God in you for sure. They go out and gun you down, and if I decide… if God gives me the strength to just surrender like that, I'll call you and all I'll do, like I said, Shari Faye's location, and, ah, when I see them drive up, and I'll see Charlie Keyes and Sheriff Metts get out of the car… they'll recognize me. I'll approach them and I'll put my hands straight up in the air and turn my back to them and they can approach me without shooting me and stuff, all right?"

"Okay."

"Okay," he continued. "Now listen carefully. Shari Faye was, ah, I'm trying to fill in all the gaps here. Shari Faye was, ah–God accepted her in Lexington County at 4:58 in the morning and… I delivered her to Saluda County, and also I told you exactly. I gave no reason to lie to you. I told you exactly how she died and so forth, and when I took the duct tape off of her, they… they… the examiner said they're having problems telling how she died…"

"Uh-huh," said Dawn as she fought a sick feeling in her stomach.

"Ah, when I took the duct tape off, it took a lot of hair with it, so that'll help 'em out."

"Where's the duct tape?" she asked.

"Only God knows, I don't... okay... now listen... now Richard, ah, okay, did you receive the thing and the pictures in the mail?"

He sounded nervous now. As much as it pained her, Dawn knew she had to reassure her sister's killer again. "They're coming." It was a lie. The family had yet to get anything.

"They... the FBI is going to intercept them... okay, it's written to you. I got Shari Faye to explain three or four different things," he said.

The suspect rambled on and on from there. He spent the rest of the call talking about Shari's relationship with Richard. He claimed she had told him that Richard was the jealous type and that she had wanted to break up with him over it. Dawn did not believe this; it seemed like just another fantasy of this man who desired a girl like Shari but knew he could not have her. The suspect talked about Robert and how Shari wanted the best for him when he grew up. Finally, he said that Shari requested that the family sing along to her favorite song on her upcoming birthday, and that she would be listening from heaven.

But all Dawn wanted to know was why he failed to turn himself in. He had talked about it so much, and then he just chickened out? "Don't you realize what you've put us through?" she snapped. "How could you think about what would happen to yourself?"

The suspect hung up not long after. Had her anger managed to scare him away? Part of her hoped it had.

Meanwhile, on the law enforcement side of things, the investigation had slowed to a crawl. This last lengthy phone call was traced to Augusta, Georgia, dozens of miles away. The FBI field office in Colombia was requesting more help from the Behavioral Science unit, finally getting them officially involved.

The FBI had already come up with a suspect profile for the killer, but gaining access to the recordings of the calls gave them further insight. Douglas writes:

"...we were now pretty sure this UNSUB was either living alone or with his parents, or perhaps an older female relative who knew nothing about his crimes.

Building on our expectation that he'd have some sort of criminal record involving sex crimes, we figured that wherever he lived, besides the pornography we'd find a hidden collection of souvenirs from his exploits: jewelry, underwear, or other personal tokens taken from his victims–including items stolen from women he'd watch as a peeping Tom earlier in his criminal career, breaking into their homes when they were out because he wasn't yet sophisticated enough to carry out an abduction."

In terms of what he might have taken, Shari's missing class ring immediately comes to mind. It would explain his insistence that he had no idea where it was, despite it having been a treasured item that Shari kept on her at all times.

Furthermore, they concluded that the suspect was likely not an unskilled laborer; his tendency to disguise his voice implied a background in electrical engineering, albeit a minor one. He was no genius, but he was not dumb either, and he seemed to think he was smarter than everyone working the case.

He was also certainly not going to kill himself. Instead, he was itching to kill someone else—and soon.

XII

The Next Girl

IT WAS JUNE 14TH, AND NINE-YEAR-OLD DEBRA May Helmick was enjoying her summer. She and her sister, Becky, and their little brother, Woody, ran around the yard in front of her family's trailer home. The Helmick family had only moved to Shiloh Mobile Home Park in Richland County about two months prior, but to little Debra May, it was already becoming a home.

Debra's mother, Debra Louise, saw her daughter at three thirty in the afternoon. She was preparing to go to work at a local restaurant and was getting a ride from a neighbor, Vicky (spelled Vickie in some sources) Orr. Not wanting to leave the kids alone, the elder Debra and Vicky decided to take them along for the drive until Debra's husband, Sherwood, returned home in the evening. Unexpectedly, however, Sherwood arrived early that day.

Soon after the two women left, an unfamiliar car drove into the park. It was a silver-colored vehicle with red racing stripes. Strangely, the car went down the park's driveway, only to make an abrupt U-turn. It stopped for a while until it slowly made its way in front of the Helmicks yard. The door swung open, and a man stepped outside.

It was by pure chance that another neighbor, nineteen-year-old Ricky Morgan, heard the screams. Despite the heat, he had the air conditioner off and his windows were open. Puzzled, he looked out only to see the unknown man grabbing Debra May by the waist while she kicked and screamed, shoving her into his car, and speeding off.

Morgan ran as fast as he could to the Helmick's trailer. He called out to Sherwood. "Did you see that man take your daughter?"

Sherwood had not. Inside the trailer, the air conditioner was droning away, masking almost all outside noise. It was then that they noticed three-year-old Woody hiding under a bush. The little boy was terrified. He sobbed. "The bad man said he was coming back to get me!"

Sherwood sped off in his car in hopes of finding the silver car. When he could not, he stopped a police car to tell them what happened. Word spread fast, and Frank Powell, the sheriff for Richland County where the trailer park was located, already had some ideas of what was happening.

There was a stark difference in age between Shari Smith and Debra Helmick, but the other similarities were obvious: both were pretty blonde girls with blue eyes. The families lived less than thirty miles away from each other. The description that Ricky Morgan gave was that of a slightly chubby, bearded, white man with a receding hairline also sounded eerily similar to the suspect Lexington County Police were still looking for. What more, Debra had been abducted exactly two weeks and within an hour after Shari had.

This information was not lost on police. If there was any chance at all that the same sick person was behind this, it meant there was no time to waste. Not long after Richland County cops were contacted, a helicopter was called in to perform an aerial search of the area.

While the search unfolded, someone needed to alert Debra Louise. She had been busy, searching the back room of Ray Lever's Bar-B-Q for cans of pork and beans, when her boss approached her. He looked worried. "Get your purse," he told her. "Your mother-in-law is coming to pick you up."

Debra Louise felt a spike of anxiety. She had not even been gone long and already something was up. What could have possibly happened? Had there been an accident at the trailer park? Was one of her children hurt? When her mother-in-law showed up, she rushed to the car and shouted for an answer.

Her mother-in-law was frantic. "Debra May has been kidnapped!"

Instantly, Debra Louise felt her fear dissipate. "Oh, that's bull," she replied. This was probably all just a ploy from her husband. He never liked the fact that she was out working and imagined that this was all probably a ruse to get her to stay home with the kids. Still, she got in the car and rode home.

This was all too strange. Her mother-in-law seemed scared, genuinely so. As they neared the Helmick trailer, the older woman was bordering on hysterics.

Any hopes Debra Louise had left that this was all just some cruel trick were dashed when she saw the crowd of neighbors gathered in front of her family's home.

Oh my God! If only Debra May had gotten into the car and ridden to work with me, she thought. Debra May would still be here!

As the only witness, the police focused their attention on Ricky Morgan. Morgan managed to provide them with a physical description: they were looking for a white male, likely in his early to mid-thirties. He stood around five feet and nine inches tall and weighed around two hundred and fifteen pounds. He had a beer belly, brown hair including a beard and mustache, and a receding hairline. Police used this information to create a composite sketch of the subject, which bore a striking resemblance to the sketch of the man who took Shari.

Morgan went into further detail. "The man was wearing white short pants and a light-colored sleeveless shirt and he had something white in his hand that looked like a bag. When he approached the children, he leaned over like he was talking to them. That's when he grabbed Debra May, and she started kicking and screaming. I saw her feet hitting the top of the car as he threw her across the seat, and then she stopped kicking."

The vehicle in question was not an Oldsmobile. Morgan believed it to have been a 1982 or 1983 Grand Prix or Monte Carlo. It had red racing stripes and South Carolina license plates.

If social tensions were running high after what happened with Shari, Richland County authorities were afraid news of this latest crime could send things over the edge. In no time at all, rumors were swirling about what happened to little Debra May and who had taken her. This was the sort of thing that could seriously hurt an investigation, hindering it before it could even really begin. Sheriff Frank Powell announced that police were going to be tightlipped moving forward, not publicly announcing any new information until it was deemed necessary.

After all, they knew someone was out there who had all that information already.

XIII

The Next Discovery

ANOTHER WAY TO TELL IF THIS WAS THE SAME man: would he make any phone calls? There was a problem there as the Helmick's had no phone. Eight agonizing days would go by without any movement on either Shari or Debra May's case. Then, on June 22nd, the Smiths got another call.

"This is a collect call from Shari Faye Smith," said the operator.

"Yes," said Dawn. What choice did she have? "I'll take the call."

"Thank you. Dawn? You know this isn't a hoax, correct? Uh, did you find Shari Faye's ring?"

"Uh, no I didn't," said Dawn. So, she realized, the suspect had not had the guts to go through with killing himself after all.

"Okay. I don't know where it is, okay? You know, uh, God wants you to join Shari Faye. It's just a matter of time. This month, next month, this year, next year. You can't be protected all the time, and you know, uh, have you heard about Debra May Helmick?"

"Richland County?"

"Yeah," he confirmed. "Go one north… well, one west, turn left at Peach Festival Road or Bill's Grill. Go three and a half miles through Gilbert, turn right, last dirt road before you come to a stop sign at Two Notch Road. Go through chain and 'No Trespassing' sign; go fifty yards and to the left go ten yards/ Debra May is waiting. God forgive us all."

Keep him on the line, she thought. "Hey, listen!"

"What?"

"Uh, just out of curiosity, how old are you?"

"Dawn E., your time is near. God forgive us and protect us all. Goodnight for now, Dawn E. Smith."

"Wait a second here! What happened to those pictures you said you were gonna send me?"

"Oh," he replied. "Apparently the FBI must have them."

"No, sir, because when they have something, we get it, too, you know. Are you gonna send them? I think you are jerking me around because you said they were coming, and they're not here."

"Goodnight, Dawn," he repeated simply. "I'll talk to you later."

It had been another painful experience, but it lasted long enough for police to trace the call to the Palmetto Plaza Shopping Center, which was located in Sumter, South Carolina, and about fifty miles away from the Smith family home. Once again, the caller left no trace of himself at the scene.

Police moved out. Just where he said, there was Debra May's body, lying in a wooded area, surrounded by trees and bushes. Like Shari, she was badly decomposed from the summer heat, but there was one thing that stood out right away: Debra was found wearing two pairs of underwear, a plain cotton pair, and a satin, bikini-style pair that seemed to belong to an adult woman.

This act of perversion made it clear: police were dealing with a psychopath the likes of which they had never seen.

The idea was driven further by the discovery of tufts of Debra May's blonde hair found scattered across the woods. Crime scene investigators found one clump of hair that still had a pink barrette attached. There was a sticky reside stuck to the hair that was later determined to have come from duct tape.

Though there was strong reason to believe that this was Debra May Helmick, the little girl's body was in such bad shape that they could not positively identify her based on sight alone. They would have to confirm her identity through an autopsy, which was performed by pathologist Dr. Erwin Shaw at Lexington County Hospital on Saturday, June 22nd, while police examined the clothing.

Advanced decomposition limited what information could be obtained through an autopsy, but Dr. Shaw concluded that Debra May, like Shari, had likely been suffocated. He also took tissue samples from her fingertips and bottoms of her feet to compare prints.

In situations like this, where soft tissues are too damaged to study closely, the teeth of the decedent can be extremely helpful. Not only do teeth contain DNA, but chemical testing can reveal much about a person's life. Isotope analysis of teeth can tell us where a person might have been born, where they spent the last few years of their life, what food they ate, and even where that food might have come from.

The most straightforward approach, however, is with X-rays. Like fingerprints, dental records are unique; no two people will have the same dental history.

The problem was that no dental records for Debra May could be provided. Whether they were lost, left behind in the Helmick family's native Ohio, or simply never taken in the first place is unknown. Investigators hit a wall. They would have to try something else.

Sheriff Metts, along with Lexington County coroner Harry Harmon, reached out to Dr. Ted A. Rathbun, a forensic physical anthropologist at the University of Southern Carolina. Dr. Rathbun could perform a craniofacial superimposition on the girl's skull, a technique that involves closely and very carefully comparing the skull to a living photograph of the deceased.

Forensic photographer Rita Schuler explains further:

In positioning for the superimposition, particular care was given to the match of anatomical features: the point of the chin, the lower nasal border, the incisor (tooth) edges, height and gap of the central and right lateral maxillary incisors (upper teeth) of both the skull and photograph. Zoom lenses attached to the cameras permitted instant adjustment of magnification of each image to a common scale. The teeth in the photograph and the teeth in the skull were an exact match. Also congruent were the openings and bridges of the nose, the size and shape of the eye sockets, distance between the eyes and the shape of the chin and the right jaw line.

Dr. Rathburn concluded: *In my professional opinion, the superimposition of the skull and the photograph is convincing evidence for the identification of the skeletal remains as those of Debra May Helmick within reasonable medical certainty.*

Meanwhile, Richland County police worked with the girl's parents. The silky bikini panties were immediately determined to have not belonged to Debra May, but the barrette was different.

"Yes, that's Debra May's," said Debra Louise after being presented with them. "Around two o'clock that day, I washed her hair, brushed it and put two pink barrettes in it. That's one of them."

On Monday, June 24th, the body was positively identified as nine-year-old Debra May Helmick.

Sheriff Metts gave a news conference where he announced that law enforcement was now working under the belief that Shari Smith and Debra May Helmick's cases were linked.

Later, Debra Louise said, "We watched the news about Shari's abduction and murder on TV, and Debra May would sit on the floor in front of the TV and listen to it and say how pretty Shari was, and how sad it was that she was killed. After the abductions were connected, all we could see on TV was Debra May's picture right there beside Shari's."

Sherwood, Debra May's father, could not bear to see his daughter's picture on the news. One night, he had enough and reportedly picked the television up and threw it out the door.

Debra May's funeral was originally meant to be held on Tuesday, June 25th, but they could not go through with it. June

25th was the birthday of Becky, their only daughter now that Debra May had been so cruelly taken from them. It was instead held the following day and was attended by the Smith family.

"This is a very difficult time for all of us," said the pastor. "We are afraid, angry, sad and broken. When will it end?"

XIV

The Break at Last

THE IDEA THAT A VICTIM COULD HELP SOLVE their own murder from beyond the grave is one with understandable appeal. It is a way for justice to come full circle, for the deceased to come back to life, if only momentarily, to put the ones who hurt them behind bars. Usually, these instances are given a supernatural explanation. Perhaps the most well-known case of justice from beyond the grave would be that of Teresita Basa, an immigrant from the Philippines who was murdered in her Chicago apartment on February 21, 1977. Her killer had undressed her, stabbed her in the chest with a large kitchen knife, and set the whole place on fire.

For months, the investigation went nowhere. That was, until Teresita's coworker, Remibias Chua, began seeing Teresita in her dreams. She thought she could hear Teresita begging her to help solve the crime. During a nap, Remibias began to speak in what sounded like Teresita's voice and stated that her killer was a hospital orderly named Allen Showery. During another episode, Teresita told them that Showery had stolen some of her jewelry.

Wouldn't you know it—an investigation found Teresita's jewelry in the possession of Showery's girlfriend. After it was confirmed that Showery had access to Teresita's apartment, he confessed to murdering her. In 1979, he was sentenced to only fourteen years in prison.

Though Shari's spirit was not pulling any dramatic stunts like this, Dawn had reason to feel that her sister was helping to solve her own murder. Everything went back to her Last Will and Testament. It was by far the most valuable piece of evidence, something that police were still hoping would reveal some obscure detail they had missed before. Among the first people to examine the letter was police lieutenant Mickey Dawson, a member of the SLED Questioned Document Unit. He had spent the night that the letter had been recovered comparing its handwriting to samples of Shari's known writing. They were a match, but there had to be something more.

That was where SLED Questioned Document Examiner Gaile Heath came in. She processed both the letter and the envelope on an Electrostatic Detection Apparatus, also known as an ESDA. Schuler explains the process:

The ESDA is an instrument that develops indented writings from paper products. It works on the opposite principle of a printing press. Instead of coating raised letters with ink to create an image, the ESDA fills in the indentations on the document in question with graphite particles called "carrier particles." When an imaging film similar to Saran Wrap is pulled tight over the document, a readable image can possibly come through, making the indentations legible in varying degrees in such a manner that the indentations may be captured in hard copy form and the information from these indentations made available for investigative use.

Studying the paper revealed something interesting: there were impressions on it, too faint to be seen by the naked eye, that were from another person's handwriting.

Shari's letter had been written on a legal pad that had been used before. There were traces of a grocery list and a phone number that was traced all the way to Huntsville, Alabama. Police called and came into contact with an older married couple, Ellis and Sharon Sheppard.

It turned out that the couple had been on vacation for several weeks and had a man who worked alongside Ellis as an electrician's assistant house-sat for them. They described him as a normal, mild-mannered man in his mid-thirties who was still living with his parents. He was divorced and had a twelve-year-old son he had no contact with. He was a good worker, very meticulous in everything he did with an eye for small details.

This man was also obsessed with Shari's murder. It was all he talked about, and he had been saving newspaper clippings from every article that mentioned it.

When Ellis heard a phone recording of the suspect's voice, he said, "That's Larry Gene Bell. No doubt about it."

The description fit Bell completely, and things were really starting to come together when police learned that Bell had been given access to the Sheppard's .38 pistol. The gun had been taken from its usual hiding place. Later, it was found beneath the mattress in the room Bell had been staying in, next to a Hustler magazine featuring a blonde woman in bondage on the cover.

The very next day, Bell was brought into police custody.

So, who exactly was Larry Gene Bell? In 1985, he was thirty-five years old and somewhat overweight, though he appeared to have lost a few pounds between the time he kidnapped Shari and his arrest. Friends and family called him Gene, and they had no reason to suspect that he was anything but a normal, law-abiding citizen. People knew him as a nice, quiet guy who liked to help others out.

They had no idea that he had been convicted of at least three violent crimes.

In 1975, he committed assault and battery with a knife on a woman in Rock Hill, South Carolina. He was supposed to have served five years for it, but the sentence was suspended, and he was let out on probation with a fine of a thousand dollars. Months later, in Columbia, he was charged with assaulting a woman he had tried to force into his car but does not appear to have served any time. In late 1979, he was arrested after he launched a harassment campaign against a ten-year-old girl, to whom he made over eighty obscene phone calls. Again, he was only put on probation for five years.

Bell has also been linked to a number of different cases involving missing women in the Charlotte, North Carolina, area dating from the 1970s to the 80s. The first woman was twenty-seven-year-old Priscilla Ann Blevins. The young woman, who had dreams of becoming a translator for the United Nations, vanished suddenly on July 7, 1975. She left her home on Tyvola Road and was never seen again. The last person to see her was her roommate. The case would go cold until 2012, when DNA taken from Blevins's sister matched with a Jane Doe whose skeletal remains had been discovered off of Interstate 40 in 1985. What exactly happened to Blevins in the time between her disappearance and the discovery of her body remains unknown.

That same month, on the 31st, twenty-one-year-old newlywed Denise Porch vanished after showing a brown-haired man around the Yorktown Apartments complex where she lived and worked as a resident manager. The Yorktown Apartments, like Blevins's home, was located on Tyvola Road. Her husband returned home from work later that day to find their apartment empty. Nothing had been taken aside from a log of vacant apartment units and their keys. Porch was a pretty blue-eyed blonde who just happened to live some three hundred yards away from Larry Gene Bell at the time. No trace of her has ever been found.

The last person to see twenty-six-year-old insurance adjuster and model Sandee Cornett was her fiancé, who had left her house on the evening of November 18, 1984, after the two had dinner together. The fiancé, who lived in South Carolina, was unable to reach Cornett by phone the following day. Neither her employer nor her parents were able to reach her, either. Nothing was stolen from Cornett's house aside from her ATM card, which was used three times in the following weeks by two still-unidentified people, a man and a woman. Cornett and Larry Gene Bell actually knew each other, though the connection was distant; they had both once attended a mutual friend's birthday party. He also lived nearby at the time.

On August 12th, Bell was indicted for Shari's kidnapping and murder by a Saluda County court, though due to some jurisdictional issues, as well as the fact that it was almost impossible to find jurors who didn't want to kill Bell themselves, the trial would not take place until February 10, 1986.

While in custody, he demanded that officials from Charlotte be brought to him. He told them, "I want to tell them some things about a missing girl named Sandee. God is going to reveal to me where Sandee Cornett's body is."

He never said anything else about the case.

During the trial, he often pretended to be insane. He rambled on about other missing girls, though always avoided answering any questions. He claimed to have had a split personality, "another" evil Larry Gene Bell that shared his body and was capable of the murder. Most shockingly, he repeatedly had outbursts where he asked Dawn to marry him. Those who attended the trial believed that he was faking mental illness, not only to potentially get a lighter sentence, but also as an excuse to further torment the families of his victims.

On February 23rd, the trial came to an end. The jury, which had deliberated for less than three hours found him guilty on all counts, and the state wanted to pursue the death penalty. The following spring, on April 2, 1987, he received another death sentence for the murder of Debra May Helmick after the jury deliberated for just over an hour.

The nightmarish ordeal had at last come to an end: Larry Gene Bell would never be able to hurt another innocent person again.

Conclusion

LARRY GENE BELL REMAINED IN THE BROAD River Correctional Institution in Columbia, South Carolina, for the next several years. He was hated by the other inmates and nicknamed the "baby killer." For his own safety, he was kept away from the general population of inmates.

In 1993, Dawn became engaged to a friend named Will Jordan. Somehow, Bell had gotten word of this and sent the couple a card. In it, he wished Dawn a happy twenty-fifth birthday. He also wished them much happiness in their marriage.

It bothered Dawn, but not as much as she thought it would. After all, this was all he could do now. He could not hurt her or anyone else she loved. She knew he was finally powerless, and that must have driven him crazy.

The Smiths did their best to go on with their lives, but there was always an emptiness, the bitter feeling of Shari's absence. Their Christian faith and their community had helped them through their darkest days, and though they learned to live with the loss, they kept her memory alive however they could. In 1995, Dawn recorded a music album dedicated to her little sister.

Bell would be executed on October 4, 1996. He was forty-six years old.

References

Smith, D. (1993) *Grace So Amazing* GSA Publishing

Douglas, J. (2022) *When a Killer Calls: A Haunting Story of Murder, Criminal Profiling, and Justice in a Small Town* Dey Street Books

Schuler, R. (2007) *Murder in the Midlands: Larry Gene Bell and the 28 Days of Terror that Shook South Carolina* The History Press

"The Disturbing Story Of Larry Gene Bell, The Depraved Killer Who Shocked Even 'Mindhunter' John Douglas" Retrieved from: https://allthatsinteresting.com/larry-gene-bell

"Larry Gene Bell" Retrieved from: https://murderpedia.org/male.B/b1/bell-larry-gene.htm

"Ret. FBI Profiler John Douglas on Larry Gene Bell, 'One of the Most Sadistic Murderers' He's Investigated" Retrieved from: https://www.aetv.com/real-crime/john-douglas-shari-smith

Acknowledgements

This is a special thanks to the following readers who have taken time out of their busy schedule to be part of True Crime Seven Team. Thank you all so much for all the feedbacks

James,

Sherry Quimby, Andrew Ayers, Shelley Specht, Kris Bowers, Sherry Whitaker, Sharron Henry, Robert Upton, LibertySusan Galsor, Angie Grafton, Amanda, Alan Kleynenberg, Alicia Gephart, Alicia Gir, Richard Allen, Alma Verster, Daurice St.Denis, Anna McCown, April Clarke, Jennifer Hanlon, Ashlynn Stinson, Alex Slocomb, Angela Brockman, Maryann Quinn, Bambi Dawn Goggio, Casey Renee Bates, Kurt Brown, Beth Alfred, Lee Fowley, Shelli Blankenbaker, Amanda, Barbara English, Bruce Weldin, Bryce Hartford, Brooke Youngs, Chad Mellor, Cara Butcher, Joyce Carroll, Allyssa Howells, Cory Lindsey, Clara Cortex, Nancy Harrison, Carrie Roberson, Joan Baker, Connie White, Dawn Winter, David Edmonds, David Helling, Dani Bigner, Awilda Roman, Donna Champion, Donna Freile, Betty May, Rebecca Donnell, Paul Kelley, Emma Futter, Marion E. M. Newman, Francis Bernardi, Larry J. Field, Linda J Evans, Diane Kourapian, Cathy Russell, Helaine Lasky, Deborah Hanson, Shannon Bruce, Toni Marie Rinella, Jessica Harvey, Huw, Angela Sims, John Edward, Ray Vertett, Jessica Bowman, Jennifer Fail, Jennie, Jo Pardoe, Wanda Jones, Jon Wiederhorn, James, Jeanine Copperstone, Judy Stephens, Laura Rouston, Laura Mish, Lissette Ortiz, Landa-Lou Goodridge, Justine, Fran Joyner, Karin Dennis, Karen A. McCabe, Kay, Jennifer Jones, Kelly Wise, Dezirae, Chandra, Michelle Simpson, Deirdre Green, Debbie Hill, Lorrie VanMeter, Leslie Rasmussen, Kimberly Herout, Sue Reutzel, Maguelonne, Marquita Leggett, Jason, Miranda Sowers, Wanda L. Michele Gosselin, Barbara Pollock, Melody Sanderson, Monica Yokel, Marcia Heacock, Underwood, Rebecca Stallman Catazaro, Jason C. Tillery, Muhammad Nizam Bin Mohtar, Tamara, Bonnie Kernene, Beverly Harris, Natalie Gwinn, Natasha Rachel B, Hoadley, Cynthia Z. Miller, Nicky McLean, Jaimie Rasmussen, Sue Wallace, Ole Pedersen, Keri Wallace, Kathy Morgan, Patricia Oliver, Amanda Gallegos, Cheryl Griffis, Paula Jackson, Lisa Bogenschneider, Stacia Lanway, Robert Fritsch, Christy Riemenschneider, Shane Neely, Lynn Butler, Rebecca Ednie, Susan Weaver, Brenda M Bennett, Ferne Miller, Tammy Sittlinger, Tamela L. Matuska, Don Price, Tane Boghozian, Tina Bullard, Daniel Thaakirah Wolfe Charles, Thomas Stewart Rae, Tina Shattuck, Marcie Walters, Brandy Noble, Tara Pendley, Jan Tweed,

Lee Batts.

Continue Your Exploration Into

The Murderous Minds

Excerpt From True Crime Solved

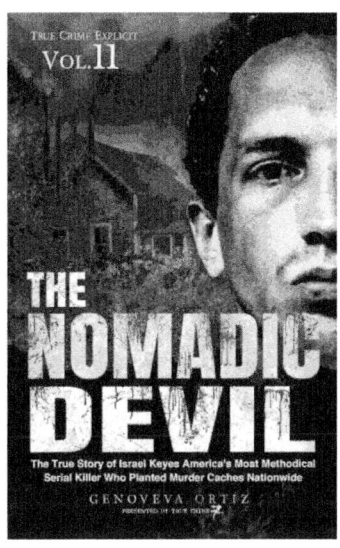

I
A Monster on the Loose

FEBRUARY 2011.

It has been a tough month for the residents of Anchorage, Alaska. Tensions have been running high since a young, female barista disappeared from a local coffee stand on the night of the 1st. The girl's family was understandably worried sick when she failed to return home after her shift, and their fear only grew when they began to receive strange text messages from her.

I'm going to my friend's house for a few days. Tell my dad I love him. You won't hear from me until I come home.

The girl's boyfriend looked at the message in confusion. Why would she suddenly leave and not take any of her belongings with her? Which friend was she staying with? Why? These were questions with no real answers, because he knew on some level that every word was a lie. He had no way to prove his suspicions, but the more days went by without another word from her, the worse his worries grew.

Posters bearing her image and information had been put up all over the area. Her father offered a twelve thousand five hundred dollar reward for information leading to the girl's return, and anyone who knew the man was sure he would have offered a lot more if he could have. He was a devoted single father, and not having her around was taking its toll on him, emotionally and physically.

On February 11th, over one thousand people attended a candlelight vigil at the town square park in downtown Anchorage. It was a touching scene, people from all over the community coming together to support the family.

Around that same time, another Anchorage resident was getting off a cruise ship near his hotel in New Orleans, Louisiana. He was well aware of the news surrounding the missing girl, but this hardly ruined his vacation. If anything, it had only made getting away all the more enjoyable. He was quite content with the knowledge that he had information others desperately wanted, and he was in no hurry to share it.

This man knew exactly where the girl was.

No, he wanted to take his sweet, sweet time. Maybe he would never tell anyone anything—it was much more fun to watch people scramble for answers that would never be found, after all.

The man passed through Dallas, Texas, on his way back to Anchorage on the 16th. Now that his trip was over, he was getting bored again. After finding a suitable location, a thirty-five hundred square-foot house and barn, he seized the opportunity to have some fun. The man set a fire and soon both buildings were up in flames.

The locals stopped in their tracks and watched as the sky turned dark with smoke. Heat warped the air. The fire was so massive that they feared it would swallow everything around it. Yet, this stranger was totally unconcerned. It was as if the flames did not even exist to him. He stopped only to ask for directions before he took off.

The man was excited to get home. On the 19th, he was back in Anchorage. His young daughter had also returned to school and his girlfriend was at work. He always enjoyed his time alone.

He went to his shed and opened the large cabinet.

Inside, lay the frozen body of the missing girl.

He carefully removed her from the drawer. She was naked except for a tarp he had wrapped around her, though even this had not prevented her from making a mess inside the cabinet. The blood from the wound on her back had soaked the insulation lining the floor. Annoyed, the man cleaned up the scene and disposed of the tarp, insulation, and what was left of the girl's clothing in his fireplace.

The rest of the day came and went. The man left the girl in the shed while he gathered the supplies needed for the next part of his plan. The return of his girlfriend the following morning did not slow him down, either. He had long ago made it clear to the woman that he did not like her interfering in his business.

He returned to the shed after a shopping trip for a camera, makeup, fishing line, and sewing needles. Among his haul was a newspaper he found in a dumpster. It was the February 13th edition, recent enough to make his plan believable.

Using the makeup, fishing line, and needles, the man set to work. It was not an easy task. Her skin had turned darker as she thawed, and the blood pooled beneath her skin. Her eyes were dull and blank, meaning they were best left closed. It took a lot of makeup and fishing line to make her look alive again.

The man snapped a few photos of her with his new camera. Then he typed up a ransom note. He had seen the news and was aware of how much money the girl's father was offering, but he decided it was not enough. He demanded at least thirty thousand dollars to be deposited in the girl's bank account in exchange for her return.

The thought of it all made him laugh.

Using the girl's phone, the man sent another text to her boyfriend, giving him directions to a park where he had left the typed note and photograph. All that was left now was to get rid of the body. Luckily, he was quite handy with a saw.

On the 21st, the man headed towards Matanuska Lake with the girl's dismembered remains in tow. He walked out onto its frozen surface and cut a hole in the ice before throwing her into the water. The body, held down by fishing weights, slowly sank to the bottom of the lake.

After a few more hours, the man packed up his belongings. He was happy to have caught a few fish and planned to cook them for his family's dinner that night.

The fun was over for now. It was time to get back to his other life.

The End of **The Preview**

Visit us at **truecrimeseven.com** or **scan QR Code using your phone's camera app** to find more true crime books and other cool goodies.

About True Crime Seven

True Crime Seven is about exploring the stories of the sinful minds in this world. From unknown murderers to well-known serial killers.

Our writers come from all walks of life but with one thing in common and that is they are all true crime enthusiasts. You can learn more about them below:

Ryan Becker is a True Crime author who started his writing journey in late 2016. Like most of you, he loves to explore the process of how individuals turn their darkest fantasies into a reality. Ryan has always had a passion for storytelling. So, writing is the best output for him to combine his fascination with psychology and true crime. It is Ryan's goal for his readers to experience the full immersion with the dark reality of the world just like how he used to do it in his younger days.

Nancy Alyssa Veysey is a writer and author of true crime books, including the bestselling, Mary Flora Bell: The Horrific True Story Behind an Innocent Girl Serial Killer. Her medical degree and work in the field of forensic psychology, along with postgraduate studies in criminal justice, criminology and pre-law, allow her to bring a unique perspective to her writing.

Kurtis-Giles Veysey is a young writer who began his writing career in the fantasy genre. In late 2018, he has parlayed his love and knowledge of history into writing nonfiction accounts of true crime stories which occurred in centuries past. Told from a historical perspective, Kurtis-Giles brings these victims and their killers back to life with vivid descriptions of these heinous crimes.

Kelly Gaines is a writer from Philadelphia. Her passion for storytelling began in childhood and carried into her college career. She received a B.A. in English from Saint Joseph's University in 2016 with a concentration in Writing Studies. Now part of the real world, Kelly enjoys comic books, history documentaries, and a good scary story. In her true crime work, Kelly focuses on the motivations of the killers and backgrounds of the victims to draw a more complete picture of each individual. She deeply enjoys writing for True Crime Seven and looks forward to bringing more spine-tingling tales to readers.

James Parker the pen-name of a young writer from New Jersey who started his writing journey with play-writing. He has always been fascinated with the psychology of murderers and how the media might play a role in their creation. James loves to constantly test out new styles and ideas in his writing so one day he can find something cool and unique to himself.

Brenda Brown is a writer and an illustrator-cartoonist. Her art can be found in books distributed both nationally and internationally. She has also written many books related to her graduate degree in psychology and her minor in history. Like many true crime enthusiasts, she loves exploring the minds of those who see the world as a playground for expressing the darker side of themselves—the side that people usually locked up and hid from scrutiny.

Genoveva Ortiz is a Los Angeles-based writer who began her career writing scary stories while still in college. After receiving a B.A. in English in 2018, she shifted her focus to nonfiction and the real-life horrors of crime and unsolved mysteries. Together with True Crime Seven, she is excited to further explore the world of true crime through a social justice perspective.

You can learn more about us and our writers at:

truecrimeseven.com/about

Get our **Bestseller for FREE on Audible** when you sign up to Audible for a free 30-Day Trial. You can cancel at any time if you don't like the experience of listening on the go. But you can keep your free book.

Sign up at: **https://geni.us/A1ce8iC**

Or **scan QR Code using your phone's camera app.**

Listen to 48 True Crime Stories Today For FREE.

For updates about new releases, as well as exclusive promotions, join True Crime Seven readers' group and you can also **receive a free book today.** Thank you and see you soon.

Sign up at: **freebook.truecrimeseven.com/**

Or **scan QR Code using your phone's camera app.**

Dark Fantasies Turned Reality

Prepare yourself, we're not going to **hold back on details or cut out any of the gruesome truths...**

Printed in Great Britain
by Amazon